ACCLAIM FOR B

Beyond Agile provides a broad but strong foundation for agile practices, but it doesn't stop there. After grounding us in solid theory, Beyond Agile takes us beyond the typical business book, diving deep into the ongoing practices of real teams doing real work. They stories bust many myths about agile and shares the human stories of real people and their struggles, trials and triumphs. Each story makes the complex and evolving topic of agile in the workplace engagingly clear and simple. Beyond Agile is a great, foundational and inspiring book.
~ Dave Gray, Author of Gamestorming and The Connected Company

For anyone who is looking to turn theory into practice in the real world, this book will be invaluable. The basic principles of continuous improvement are not complicated, and they are presented here in a practical straightforward style. But the real world tends to be messier The Tales of Continuous Improvement presented in this book have already led me to a deeper understanding of how to put the principles into practice, and how to cultivate a culture of continuous improvement in my company. I cannot recommend it highly enough.
~ Chris Hefley, CEO, LeanKit

This is a rich set of case studies with useful snippets from teams that have moved along the scrum/kanban path. Real examples we can use for practical implementation in our own organisations. Use it to increase your knowledge and improve discussions within your teams. The new 'must have' to expedite through your reading backlog.
~ Kim Ballestrin, Agile Engagement Lead, Telstra

The case studies in this book are inspiring examples of how brave and honest people can apply principles of continuous improvement and overcome the confusion, fear, and waste that get in the way of flow. A very engaging read. ~ Darrell Damron, Washington State Governor's Office of Accountability and Performance - WA State Lean Community of Practice Lead

Having been intimately involved for the past decade and more in helping people understand continuous improvement and the flow of value in software development, this book is a godsend.

Its ten real-world, warts'n'all stories illustrate Rightshifting in action - the challenges and the benefits both.

I have no doubt that through this excellent book, readers will come away wi an increased awareness of what some teams and organisations are doing—and learning—in their journey towards HESPO—the highly effective software product organisation. ~ Bob Marshall - http://flowchainsensei.word-press.com/

We all know Albert Einstein's famous quote "In theory, theory and practice are the same. In practice, they are not." This is exactly why we need this book by Jim, Maritza and Joanne! All the stories demonstrate that the ideas of Flow can have a great impact on our daily work. But the implementations look completely different, and that is okay. The world is not black and white, and the case studies give us plenty of examples how success in the real world can look like. I really enjoeyed reading this practical book and found lots of inspirations for my own work. ~ Arne Roock, IT-Agile, Brickel Key Award Winner

BEYOND AGILE

Tales of Continuous Improvement

Modus Cooperandi Press

A Division of Modus Cooperandi, Inc

1900 West Nickerson, Suite 116-88

Seattle, WA 98119

ISBN 978-0-9890812-1-4

BEYOND AGILE

Tales of Continuous Improvement

by

Maritza van den Heuvel
Joanne Ho
Jim Benson

First Edition, April, 2013

Cover Photo taken at Noho, NYC by Tonianne DeMaria Barry

Perfection is achived

not when there is nothing to add,

but when there is nothing to take away.

~ Antoine de Saint-Exupery

ACKNOWLEDGEMENTS AND THANKS

There are a number of people to thank for their direct and indirect contributions to realizing our vision for this book.

First and foremost, thanks go to the many story contributors. Thank you for generously allowing us a peek into your organizations. Your willingness to share your hard-won lessons has contributed directly to the ever-growing pool of data from organizations that have created value sustainably with the principles of flow, continuous improvement and visualization of work.

To our families: For two long years we have toiled across the boundaries of time and geography, chipping away at raw marble relentlessly until, at last, we could discern the shape of this book as we had not even imagined it when we started. Thank you for allowing us to steal time from you to give to this book.

To our friends: To Corey Ladas, for first penning Scrumban and giving us something to write about. You have inspired many organizations to find adopt flow-based approaches to work. To Fisher S. Qua, for being the most able and willing production assistant we could've asked for. Without you, this book would not be Done. To those of you who assisted with various levels of editing and reviewing: Annerine Visser, John Clapham, Troy Plant, and Leanne Lambrechts. Many thanks for

TABLE OF CONTENTS

INTRODUCTION

SECTION 1 GETTING STARTED

SECTION 2 - GRAPPLING WITH SPECIFICS

SECTION 3   GOING DEEPER

INTRODUCTION
WHAT CONTINUOUS IMPROVEMENT LOOKS LIKE

▷ **"The thing I have learned at IBM is that culture is everything."**

~ *Louis V. Gerstner, Jr., former CEO IBM*

When Gerstner said "culture is *everything*," he meant ***everything***. The processes, team makeup, conflict resolution, risk tolerance, logic, propensity to innovate, interpersonal dynamics, collaboration, benefits packages, logo, carpet … *everything*. By its very nature, everything is big. Impossibly big, in fact. So when leaders set out to create a corporate culture that will encourage a highly functional, profitable, and sustainable operation, they have a lot to think about.

There are three common approaches to cultural change that have been attempted in the past:

(1) **Stalin Model** Attempt to figure out the best way for everyone to act and impose rigid processes to ensure that everyone always acts that way.

(2) **Absentee Landlord Model** Provide no guidance or structure whatsoever, leaving responsibilities largely undefined.

(3) **American Model** Every time an emergency arises, create a new policy for it, resulting in a large number of conflicting policies that ultimately confuse and stymie the work force.

Unfortunately, these are not mutually exclusive. We've seen companies have all three of these models in action concurrently—often led by a small army of expensive consultants. The common effects of these three models are confusion, fear, and waste. Each model, in its own way, leaves staff afraid to act due to reprisal.

In this book, we examine ten companies that have adopted practices of continuous improvement. The teams we look at have had direct control of their own processes, and, over time, improved them without direct demands from those higher up the chain of command. The teams, impelled by nothing more than their sense of profession- alism, invented better processes, improved staff morale, saved money, reduced waste, lowered attrition, increased quality, and reduced risk. They did this as a byproduct of being professionals—not due to a multi-million dollar process or cultural change initiatives.

WHAT IS "SCRUMBAN"?

In 2008, Corey Ladas released his seminal white paper called "Scrumban" which was then lengthened into a book by the same name. This portmanteau of Scrum (an iterative software development methodology) and Kanban (a tool to view and manage workflow) examined Corey's transition from iterative software development to flow-based software development. It did not combine Scrum and Kanban, and it did not actively promote one methodology over another.

What the Scrumban book *did* do was to show the impact that both iterative and flow-based systems have on work. Overall, the book gave software developers options and showed how the field of software development had been evolving.

PURPOSE OF THIS BOOK

One of the constant criticisms of all management styles and fads is that they seldom come with real in-the-field case studies. This is true of any existing system: Scrum, SixSigma, Team Medicine, 5s, or what have you. This is because business management is not a science; it is an art. It is contextual. Application of the art can look scientific, but it is not.

After Corey Ladas' *Scrumban* in 2008, David Anderson's *Kanban* in 2009, and Jim Benson and Tonianne DeMaria Barry's *Personal Kanban* in 2010, we noticed that we were receiving "success stories" from around the world. But rather than the typical success stories that routinely apply best practices to a simple problem—these stories were deeper. They were stories of success through trial and error. They were success stories through painful lessons.

This book provides raw case studies of teams following both iterative and flow-based systems. These teams were inspired by either Scrumban itself or the conversations it spawned. This book does not provide repeatable examples of projects that were easy. It does not tell stories of brilliant Kanban pyrotechnics that instantly solve problems. Indeed, the tools used "solved" no problems at all. It is the application of principles by thoughtful practitioners who were honest with themselves and their organizations. When things were bad, they recognized it and dealt with it.

These are REAL real-world examples. A few of the case studies, like BrainStore, did not make it. They learned, they improved, and they closed shop. This is a fact of business. Most do not make it. The difference here: heroes like the people at BrainStore go on to innovate another day in their next entrepreneurial effort.

EIGHT PRINCIPLES OF CONTINUOUS IMPROVEMENT

Let's be clear right from the start of this section: It is titled "Eight Principles of Continuous Improvement." It is not titled "THE Eight Principles of Continuous Improvement."

Why?

Because continuous improvement demands that we recognize that finite statements invariably are proven wrong. There are always additions and exceptions. Defining THE Eight would only invite someone to say we were "wrong" because they came up with the ninth. In reality, we were not wrong; they simply came up with another. Everything in this book, like everything in every other product ever created, can be improved upon.

This is why, even when we create a business process that works, it still needs to be scrutinized. Contexts change and our processes must adapt.

WHY ARE PRINCIPLES IMPORTANT?

▶ **"Any fool can make a rule, and any fool will mind it."** *~ Henry David Thoreau*

▶ **"Rules are not necessarily sacred, principles are."** *~ Franklin D. Roosevelt*

▶ **"The principle is competing against yourself. It's about self-improvement, about being better than you were the day before."** *~ Steve Young*

When we talk about principles, we need to first examine rules. We have a love-hate relationship with rules. When people are given a rule, they examine it in selfish terms. They conform to it as minimally as possible, co-opt it, or kill it. In essence, they ask three questions:

(1) What is the least amount I can do to conform to this rule?

(2) How can I use this rule to make my life better?

(3) How can I make this rule go away and not bother me again?

That seems pretty pessimistic.

Rules are objects of control and people don't like to be controlled. What they do like is clear direction and we've been taught that rules supply this. So we'll actually ask for rules, then undermine them. In the end, rules are zero-sum games. You either conform to them (*win!*) or break them (*lose!*).

When the rule you have made with its win-lose trade-off comes up against another rule's win-lose trade-off, we get negative gaming behavior, rules exploitation, and political battles. Since context changes, the context under which rules were made changes—making the rules either irrelevant or increasingly inapplicable.

So we have psychology playing against the formulation of rigid rules.

Principles, on the other hand, are able to do what we originally intended with rules (to provide guidelines for behavior), but provides it in a flexible way, so people can adapt to changing contexts. More importantly, principles are enforced socially, where rules are enforced legally. A socially collaborative principle-based system, once established, is more stable than a rules-based system because the entire organization is empowered to enforce (and question) the principles.

Rules are also more costly to manage than principles. *Why?* In Lean manufacturing, inventory is seen as waste. Say, for example, that I like jelly beans. Each day I eat some jelly beans. So I go out and buy 60,000 tons of jelly beans because they are on sale at Costco. Now, I have to get a warehouse to store my jelly beans, I need to hire armed guards to protect them from thieves, and I need workers to keep the jelly beans dry and free of dust. The more of something you have on hand, the more you have to manage it—whether it is parts, completed products, or even candy. The simple existence of the inventory costs money.

It makes much more sense to keep the right amount of inventory on hand. One jar of jelly beans sits on the counter, doesn't go stale, and requires no additional staff. At all times, we want only the amount of inventory on hand that allows us to get our work done—and no more.

Rules can also be seen as inventory. The static, dictatorial nature of rules means that you are constantly spending money enforcing them and arguing for their existence. People need to be put in charge of the rules and those people become mired down in their adjudication. At that point, power in the company becomes unevenly distributed because someone has control of the rule.

The social and cultural nature of principles spreads out that authority and therefore reduces the inventory. Rules are man-made and usually overkill for our goals.

DEFINING OUR EIGHT PRINCIPLES

In these case studies, we will show how each team invoked some of these principles. Not all of them, mind you. Again, these eight aren't the ingredients for an instant sustainability potion. Also, these eight principles are detailed in Corey Ladas' book *Scrumban*. Here they are distilled.

Flow Delivers Value

Flow for teams is when work is flowing smoothly through any system—bottlenecks, constraints, and other elements of waste have been eliminated. It's both a sign that our processes are working and a reward.

Teams in a project produce value through a series of production steps known as a value stream. The value stream is a primary element of any work visualization technique. For example, a value stream for a hiring process might look like this:

▶ **Candidates -> First Screen -> Second Screen -> First Interview ->
Second Interview -> Selection**

When visualized, the flow of work and its components bring clarity through context. Teams see how work is being done, pinpoint where there are inefficiencies, and begin to understand what can be done about them. As flow is improved, team morale, throughput, and quality are likewise improved.

Limit Work in Progress

A team cannot complete more work than it can actually process. A person who is overloaded cannot provide full attention to the task at hand. Given that both teams and the individuals that comprise them need to pay attention to create a quality product, routinely overloading them with work reduces quality, increases re-work and creates costly bottlenecks. Limiting Work-in-Progress (WIP) allows individuals and teams to focus both on quality and completion.[1]

When teams have a WIP limit, they must finish an item currently in WIP before the customer can pull a new item of work. New work is triggered by an opening in capacity. So, if a team has a WIP of three and there are currently three things in-process, no further work can begin until one of them is complete. Likewise, if a team has too much work in its backlog, it will never be completed.

Demand, in this case, pulls from supply; the supply of labor (team capacity) determines how much work of quality can actually be done. Exceed a team's capacity and you suffer quality and timeliness degradation.

Reduce Waste and Find Effectiveness

Many Lean schools of thought over-focus on this and make it the only principle of Lean. In most cases, waste reduction is a by-product of a flow-based system. Successful and innovative teams reduce waste and find effectiveness as a matter of course. They apply best practices not by rote, but thoughtfully. They optimize for their project and are not forced to follow practices set down firm-wide. They focus on metrics, but they also relentlessly scrutinize processes in real-time. They don't wait for lagging metrics to show them failure after it has already become costly.

---

1   *Benson, Why Limit WIP, (Seattle, Modus Cooperandi Press, 2013)*

Types of waste they may seek out are:

⇨   Overproduction

⇨   Too much inventory

⇨   Bottlenecks

⇨   Rework

⇨   Over planning

⇨   Early commitment

⇨   Unnecessary movement

⇨   Leverage Craftsmanship

As work becomes more complex, we will continue to have internal experts and heroes arise. Becoming reliant on them creates inefficiencies and potential crises, should a hero or expert unexpectedly leave the project. However, it would be unwise to believe that modern production can happen entirely with a generalist workforce. Shrewd application of heroes and experts can provide great benefits.

Plan for Throughput

Heavy up-front planning, premature commitment of resources, or premature commitment to a schedule lead to stress on the project team, unrealistic expectations in the customer, and ultimately unnecessary failure. Teams that understand their actual rate of production (throughput), the variability in their work load, and the value of slack in their system, can make more reliable estimates, produce better quality work, and react to change with less upheaval.

Freedom of Association

Companies are made up of professionals. Professionals spend most of their day, every day, thinking about the work they do. Nothing is more frustrating for a professional than unnecessary roadblocks to a job well done. Organizational charts that restrict freedom of association slow professionals down and reduce value. When professionals have direct communication with their colleagues, they will find the fastest path to value creation.

Respecting Professionalism

People and the teams they comprise make better decisions when they feel their decisions are respected. The fact that these professionals have been hired to do specific work implies that they have the skills necessary to do that work and understand the implications of that work. Respect for their professionalism rests on providing workers with the information, resources, and freedom of action necessary to define their own processes and redefine them as context demands, explore collaborative relationships with other teams (even if they are in another business silo), improve as needed, and select their work as they have the capacity to do a quality job. In this way, respecting professionalism is an explicit indication of trust between management and those who are managed.

Emergent Design

Design of process is emergent; it is driven by context. The thoughtful application of process changes by the self-aware team or organization keeps process current. If process doesn't keep pace, it becomes irrelevant or even dangerous. Continuous improvement drives the design of our process, constantly evolving and adapting. The understanding that old process is quite often outdated process is vital for knowledge work.

Pull Governs

Demand pulls from supply. When there is an ability to perform work (when resources are available), the customer demanding work can pull. This can be confusing because kanban backlogs make it appear that the team members are pulling work. Ultimately, the customer demands value and that value is realized when there is capacity in the value stream. We tend to confuse the traditional roles of Product Owners, Project Managers, and other internal agents as the populators of a team's backlog. In an ideal world, however, work is generated by the demands of customers and then given form by the "productization machine" in the organization.

When work is done in a pull system, items are created at a speed that yields optimal output at a sustainable pace, because people are working as fast as possible without kicking into overdrive. If you look at the microcosm of the team's workflow, teams seem to pull their work from the backlog. This is because the supply in the backlog for many teams usually comes in at a speed above their processing speed. At this point, the team "demands" work and pulls from the "supply" in the backlog. This is a helpful way of envisioning a team's work. However, the team should realize that its work is always being "pulled" by the customer. The team are merely sequencing work to provide the highest value.

Clarity Drives Improvement

W. Edwards Deming gave the world his "Theory of Profound Knowledge." In this set of four principles, Deming was defining the building blocks for personal, team, and organizational clarity. Clarity is an essential ingredient for improvement, for it is only through seeing and understanding the system that you can change it.

The four elements of Deming's theory are:

Acknowledge the System—This is the foundation of systems thinking and makes us aware that our teams and organizations are systems. As such they have explicit and implicit rule sets that define how individuals and groups react. A common thread in Deming's writing was that if we want to change people's behavior, we should change our systems to suit. In this he was saying that when we build bad systems, bad behavior inevitably results. Professionals will either conform to the bad system or rebel against it, usually in unproductive ways. When we acknowledge the system, we admit the power of systems and begin to look critically at the systems around us.

Knowledge of Variation—We need to understand the role of variation in our work. Knowledge workers earn their money by being able to navigate some pretty choppy professional waters. There is natural variation on our work. The variation in our work means that specific estimates for effort, completion times, or costs are not only difficult, but misleading. While manufacturing Lean seeks to find standard work in the hopes of drastically reducing variation, knowledge work is much better served understanding the nature of the variation and learning to work within it. Understanding the role of variation in our work allows us to not only anticipate it, but to examine it explicitly and statistically.

Theory of Knowledge—When we begin to learn about systems, we encounter metacognition—we begin to learn about how we learn. Deming understood that learning organizations were more sustainable. As teams use tools like Kanban to critically examine how they work, they learn individually and as a group how they learn. As this understanding grows, teams get a great deal of clarity around how the team is impacted by policies, information (or lack thereof), levels of work, philosophical issues, etc. That clarity directly drives not only improvement, but the depth of experiments run to find improvement.

Understanding Psychology—When we understand the systems in which we operate and the way we and our teams learn, we begin to see into the psychology of the team and the system. Additional study by groups or group members into psychology helps us build systems that have actual chances of success. Each time we build a system—be it the value stream in Kanban, the structure of a set of teams, or the design of a software product—we are building an entity that will interact with people.

As teams interact with Deming's Theory of Profound Knowledge, especially in a visual way, they gain clarity of purpose (team, individual, product, and organization), clarity of execution (value stream, backlog, rate of work, quality, defects, bottlenecks, points of predictable failure, failure demand, etc.), and clarity of policy (the type, effectiveness, and impacts of rules currently in place that govern the production of work). This clarity highlights inefficiencies that, by their very existence, drive a self-aware organization to kaizen events or self-improvement.

WHAT TO DO WITH PRINCIPLES

▶ **"Kanban is not a process. Kanban is a practice that embodies a principle. Kanban is a mechanism that will always be specific to the problem at hand and the resources available."** *~ Corey Ladas "Scrumban"*

Corey's Scrumban concept was an illustration of the gradual movement from one process style to another; in this case moving from iterative systems to flow-based systems. The specific transition from Scrum to Kanban was mostly incidental but served as a salient example for the intended audience. The key to the system was having greater team awareness facilitated by a visual control.

For software teams working to find a process that worked in their context, Kanban served as a call to action, and at the same time a signal about the state of the system. Agile techniques of the 1990s and 2000s did an excellent job of placing software teams in a position of being able to do this self-exploration at all. Prior to the coining of the term "Agile," a number of the teams were at best managed in engineering-style planning exercises and at worst dealing with day-to-day whims of those that controlled their backlogs.

Agile changed that context. XP and later Scrum packaged pre-existing but previously unconnected concepts like batching, better communication, faster delivery cycles, and some avenues for introspection. However fundamental flaws in the Agile techniques often resulted in wastes like:

⇨   **Over-processing:** Limited and prescriptive processes that work in some contexts, not all;

⇨   **Bottlenecks:** Product Owner role concentrates client communication channels to a single person; and

⇨   **Waiting:** During an iteration, teams and business must wait to introduce new work into the system.

The adoption of Agile methods significantly improved the state of software development worldwide. It was a logical and necessary process evolution. The original Scrumban essays were based on the principles of Lean manufacturing, devised over decades by people like Deming, Ohno, Toyoda, Shingo and Womack, to name a very few.

While the Agile manifesto stressed its foundation as a set of principles, XP, Scrum, and future additions by people like Mike Cohn and Alistair Cockburn set down specific practices to follow. The growth in practices began to undermine the principles. While the rhetoric of Agile continued to stress the principles, the practices began to overshadow them, especially the principle of individuals and interactions over tools and processes. This led to the creation of dogma that held certain aspects of Agile as sacred (e.g. timeboxing, Product Owners, or test-driven development).

The great Lean thinkers have downplayed specific practices in favor of cultivating the understanding of principles, but Lean has found similar pitfalls. Through SixSigma, A3, and 5s, good ideas have been converted to industry dogma that stymies continuous improvement.

It should be clear here to anyone that both Lean and Agile have a tremendous amount of good ideas. We simply have suffered from a drive of over-standardization in both arenas. Together, Lean and Agile ideas provide a fertile ground of tools we can use to solve specific process needs.

Good decision-making should be based on principles. We can use tools to solve problems and make decisions. Where we run into problems is when we identify specific tools or procedures that can never change. Nothing in this world is eternal—especially not business process.

WHY THIS BOOK'S STRUCTURE IS WHAT IT IS

▶ **You are what you is, you is what you am...** ~ *Frank Zappa*

From here on out, practitioners tell their stories. When you read each story, keep in mind those principles described above. No story is indicative of all the principles. We do not painstakingly show how each story describes all the principles because, simply, none of them do. Just as there are eight there out of an unknown number of possible principles, no story embodies all eight.

What we start to find when we delve into the management of knowledge work, is that it is highly susceptible to variation. That variation isn't only in the type, duration, complexity, or location of the work—it is everything. Successful teams do not, in any way, have to adhere to all eight principles. Again, they are not success criteria. They have no specific applications; you have to apply them according to your context.

We have divided this book into three sections: Pursuit, Specifics, and Actual Use. Each part comes with a short overview of the stories it contains. You can choose to read each Part (or even story) independently. However, if this is all new to you, you will benefit most by starting with Part I and making your way through.

Part 1: GETTING STARTED These stories give an overview of what it feels like to pursue a flow-based environment. The changes in context, surprises in thinking, epiphanies, failures, and emotions in moving from one system to another. These stories give you real-world examples of some benefits and the challenges faced by practitioners.

Part 2: GRAPPLING WITH SPECIFICS These stories illustrate *specific* hurdles in moving from an iterative to a flow system. While this is (still) not a recipe book for implementation, these are some issues you may want to consider in the context of your own deeper understanding of flow.

Part 3: GOING DEEPER These stories show flow-based systems in operation. These systems are working, generating information, and helping the organization create quality product. Some of the stories in this section illustrate radical people-focused management practices and that even flow is not a cure-all.

Happy Reading,

Jim Benson
Seattle, WA
February, 2013

SECTION 1
GETTING STARTED

The stories in Part One illustrate what it may feel like as you set out on a journey towards continuous improvement based on the principles of flow-based (Lean/Kanban) work. Whatever your industry or the size of your team, these stories will show you how others have begun using flow-based principles and practices to kickstart change.

Changing Organizations, One Team at a Time is the story of a small software testing team making the transition from a linear (Waterfall) development approach to using iterations, and subsequently a flow-based approach, while other neighboring teams continue using their linear approaches—at least, initially.

In *Agile Automotive* we recount the experiences of WIKISPEED, an unusual automotive company that has been using every possible advantage from Scrum and Kanban from day one to build an ambitious dream: a low-cost, road-legal commuter car using one family's savings and the enthusiasm and passion of a world-wide network of volunteers.

At Getty Images, a software development team within a media company, initiated a transition from Waterfall to Scrum because they were struggling to deliver a problematic and overdue product. Their *Good Migrations* eventually inspired company executives to implement an enterprise-wide adoption of these practices, embedding them in the culture through organization-wide training and ongoing coaching.

ONE TEAM AT A TIME
Changing Organizations at Attachmate Corporation

Vital Statistics

Company: Attachmate Corporation
Location: Seattle, Washington State, United States
Industry and Domain: Software Development, Host connectivity systems, Security management
Insights by: Dawn Hemminger. Test Engineer and Technical Team Lead.

Dawn Hemminger is a Software Test Lead at Attachmate in Seattle, WA. Her experience as an engineer at Boeing in the early '90's served as her first introduction to lean manufacturing principles. Years later, after switching careers, she successfully applies these same principles to software development. When not evangelizing kanban and Lean practices at Attachmate, you can find Dawn at Seattle Lean Coffee (#sealean) most Wednesday mornings, organizing her community to create a new park, or running the beautiful trails of the Pacific Northwest.

Background

Attachmate's XTest team is small and dynamic, consisting of three to four members, depending on the specific tasks in their backlog. Having worked closely together for four years, the group is tightly knit and highly experienced (the average software development tenure of each member is upwards of ten years).

This story covers the period from January 2010 to May 2011, a time that included both personnel and structural changes as team members left and XTest merged with another team. Presently, the team continually tests Attachmate® Reflection® X and Reflection® X Advantage products throughout their release cycles. The team performs all aspects of testing from developing, monitoring and maintaining more than 30 nightly automated test projects for the product's major functional areas to exploratory testing to Electronic Product Delivery and CD verification.

The team is part of the Test Organization, which is a branch of the Engineering Department that also contains the Software Development team. While the XTest team follows agile and lean processes with influence from XP and kanban, the wider engineering team, including Development, Product Management, Technical Writers and Localizers, follow a more traditional waterfall approach.

Study Overview

Since 2008, the XTest team used physical index cards to prioritize and manage workflow. Initially, the team used an Agile-style storyboard where cards were simply pushed along. Over the years, use of the cards evolved. Now, the team uses a kanban board in which task-oriented cards are pulled along. This change better reflects present reality and the way work actually flows through the team.

During the time period covered by this story, use of their kanban-based system was limited exclusively to the three XTest team members and a few others temporarily working in the group (such as testers from other product teams or developers assigned to short test projects). Outside of the XTest team, no other members of the product department used a kanban board or any alternate type of work visualization tool. Subsequently, adoption of kanban has grown across the Engineering Department in response to the successes achieved by the XTest team.

Original Problem—Overwhelming Work in Progress

The XTest team's story began a few years ago when the team lead at-the-time encouraged his small group to embark on an ambitious, if slightly deviant, journey to transition away from the predominant waterfall methods used elsewhere in the Engineering Department (Development, Program Management, Technical Writing) and toward a testing approach that relied on the principles and tools of Lean, Agile and XP. Although the XTest team's transition occurred in isolation, team members provided status updates to the other functional areas of the Engineering

BEYOND AGILE

Department through weekly status meetings, email correspondence and hallway conversation.

The XTest team set up its very first kanban board in a small hallway by repurposing a large cork board and whiteboard. The cork board served as a shared testing backlog while the white board established a simple workflow with columns for Ready, Doing and Done. Each team member was allocated a discrete row in the Doing column with a Work-in-Progress limit of two tasks per person.

Among the early steps in the XTest team's transition included changing the way it set testing schedules. The Reflection X and Reflection X Advantage products released major updates every eight to twelve months, with six month service pack updates and monthly fixes of emergent and critical issues. Prior to its

BOARD OMNIPRESENCE

Locate your board where it can be seen. The kanban is an information radiator, if people cannot see it, then they cannot interact with it.

agile transformation, the XTest team participated in this same cycle. Once the team moved away from the waterfall methods employed elsewhere in the Engineering Department, it became necessary to reconfigure how information about upcoming features was shared.

To accomplish this transfer of information, the XTest team began holding monthly planning meetings with the Development teams. Based on what they learned from the Development teams, the XTest members created stories to support testing of these new features while simultane-ously designing stories for their own internal automation projects. Each of these story types were estimated using T-shirt sizes[1] and put in the backlog. The XTest team would then spend time and effort prioritizing the stories and identifying tasks for the most important ones. The XTest team chose to start with week-long sprints that began with a planning meeting every Monday morning and concluded with a group retrospective every Friday afternoon.

The regular planning and retrospective meetings raised a number of difficulties that prevented the team from mak-ing as much headway as they expected with this initial foray into using agile methods:

⇨ Team members spent a significant amount of time trying to write stories with supporting tasks and estimating how long it would take for stories to be completed.

⇨ Story estimates were seldom accurate and trying to task out each story was always a struggle.

⇨ When the team attempted to calculate velocity, it found the exercise to be too time-consuming and as a result kept them from coming up with an accurate enough number to help plan sprints accurately.

⇨ Many members of the team became frustrated when they were unable to complete stories within the estimated time. The team would meet every Monday morning to generate new stories even if

---

1   *An estimation technique where a feature is assigned a simple size measurement based on T-Shirt sizes, e.g. XS (very small),S, L, M, XL and XXL (very large).*

there were still tasks sitting in the **Ready** column from the previous sprint.

Watching the stories and tasks pile up until there was no more room left in the large space allocated for the backlog soon became visually overwhelming and entirely demotivating.

Objectives—To Create a Real Motivational Tool

The team wanted to keep the task board. It allowed them to effectively visualize and represent the work they wanted to do, the work they were currently doing and the work they had completed. However, the team soon realized that it needed a new way to use the tool so that tasks and stories could move more quickly to the **Done** column. This need necessitated a change to the way they generated the backlog so that tasks didn't pile up and could move into the **Doing** column faster. In addition, the team wanted the board to be more accessible and visible, not only to themselves, but also to their supporting teams.

> **IMPROVEMENT THROUGH OBSERVATION**
>
> *This was a critical step for Attachmate to engage in improvement....They began with a set of procedures that they thought would work. As they watched their work flow (or not flow) through the board, they discovered that "ideal" is a moving target. By observing "what works well in our context," rather than "doing it by the book," they were able to sculpt a working process.*

In short, the team needed to come up with a way to use the task board to better reflect the way they actually work, not how they thought they should be working.

A Tale of Gradual Improvement

The need for change became even more pressing as the team size reduced from six to three over a six-month period toward the end of 2009. With fewer people on the team, work priorities began to shift, and the need to collaborate with and rely on outside teams for help increased. It quickly became evident to the remaining three team members that their processes had to change and that the board had to be more accessible to those outside of the team who would be collaborating with them.

Almost immediately upon reaching consensus about these changes, the team moved its task board from the narrow hallway into a more dynamic and visible space— the team's pairing room. This is a public room where the team happened to spend most of its day. Initially, the board remained inconspicuous. Apart from the odd member of another team who would offer a comment or inquire as to its purpose, no one seemed to pay it much attention. To get a fresh start, the team decided to cull the original backlog. The new backlog (renamed **Input Queue**) included only the work the team knew it was going to be able to accomplish in a given sprint. All remaining stories and tasks not considered "doable" or essential were left off the board.

In addition to culling the backlog and moving the board, the team stopped writing stories and switched to populating its **Input Queue** exclusively with tasks. This change eased the stress of writing user stories and kept the team from languishing over estimations. Prior to adopting the new practices, all tasks on the board were one color, making it hard to prioritize the **Input Queue**. To address this, the team introduced color-coding for different types of tasks. For example, blue for bugs that need to be verified, green for automation test projects, white for administrative tasks, purple for customer requests and pink for failures or bugs in the automated test system. The different colors made it easier to categorize work, visually see the priorities and pull work tasks based on their relative importance. For instance, if a product release was imminent, the team would prioritize the blue bug verification tasks higher than new automated test projects and pull those blue cards into their **Doing** column first.

Within a few weeks of switching exclusively to a task-based board, team members found it difficult to independently sift through the **Input Queue** to find items that were actually ready to be worked on. The need for a filter triggered the introduction of a **Ready** column. Instead of the team's usual Monday planning meetings, they decided to set aside time during the Monday standup meeting to pull items from the **Input Queue** into the **Ready** column that they considered to be the highest priority for the week and that they felt they could accomplish during the week. Subsequently, replenishing the **Ready** column if it was running low quickly became a standard practice during daily standups. This incremental shift was a small but important change, as it ensured a continuous flow of high priority work through the system.

The team started keeping its **Input Queue** size under control by only generating detailed new tasks once existing ones were complete. Tasks that could be implemented at a later date were still added to the **Input Queue** as to not lose sight of the idea. Instead of keeping them directly on the board, overflow tasks were kept in stacked clips (one for each colored card) on the far left of the board. With the stacked task clips, the team has built in an early warning indicator that work is not moving effectively across the board or that too much work is being generated. These constraints proved vital when the team began to institute Work-in-Progress limits.

> ## CLARITY MEANS COHERENCE
>
> *Organizing your visual tools is important. An uncluttered board provides a more coherent visualization. Organized visual tools are more likely to show coherent bottlenecks, stale tickets, and poor flow. They are also more easily interpreted by non-team members*

The Team Board—A Snapshot

The team Kanban board is set up on a simple cork board and divided into five states: **Input Queue, Planning/ Analysis, Ready, In Work,** *and* **Done**. Work moves from left to right. At the left is the **Input Queue** which contains the backlog of work items for the team's products. Time sensitive tasks have the due-date posted on the right corner and are prioritized accordingly within the queue. The Development team reviews all cards in the queue during a monthly planning meeting.

Any member of the testing team can generate work items at any time. The work items represent all of the team members' day-to-day work, with the exception of personal administrative tasks and the daily bug verification that all team members are responsible for.

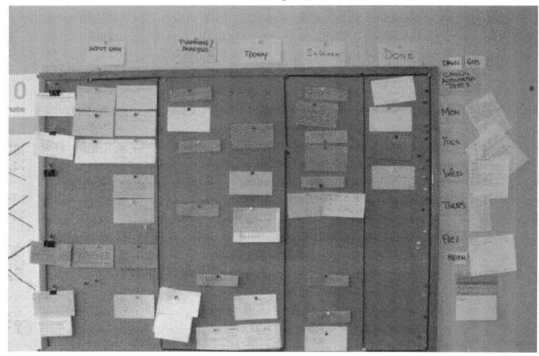

The way the team creates bug verification tasks has become a particularly flexible part of the process. Usually, only bugs that need to be verified in a timely manner (i.e. within the next week) or are high-profile become tasks on the board. Each team member is responsible for daily monitoring of their own bug verification list. If bug verification takes longer than half-an-hour, the team member may directly assign themselves a task card to indicate to the team that they're working on a specific bug. However, this is a flexible rule. Team members can create separate work item cards for each bug verification task only if doing so helps them monitor their work flow.

Prioritization of cards occurs in the column immediately before **Ready**. Any person in the team can take a task and place it under his or her name in the **Planning/Analysis** column. In this phase, the card is broken into smaller tasks, if necessary, and prioritized to be pulled into the Ready column. Work in the **Planning/Analysis** column may also return to the **Input Queue** if it is deprioritized for some reason.

All task cards in the **Ready** column are prioritized and ready to be worked on by any team member. Tasks are self-assigned. Work may be completed in pairs, since pair work has been an integral part of the team's practices since adopting an agile approach. However, the team member who pulled the task is the one responsible for making sure the task is completed.

The *In Work* column represents the tasks currently being worked on by each team member, with horizontal separators for each team member. The Work in Progress (WIP) limit per person is 2. This limit covers both the **Planning/ Analysis** and **In Work** columns. The **Ready** column is constrained physically by the number of cards that can fit vertically in the column.

After a task is complete, the team members track their emotional response to the task by drawing an emoticon on the card before placing it in the **Done** column. A smiley meant the team member was happy with the task, a flat-face meant they were ambivalent, sad meant sad, and so on. Since they were hand drawn, the emoticons could get quite expressive.

During Monday stand up meetings, the team uses the collected emoticon cards to talk about how they are feeling and to identify any improvements that could be made to make similar tasks more pleasant in the future. The Monday standup therefore doubles as both a planning meeting for the week, and an informal Retrospective of the previous week.

Tasks that are problematic or obstructing progress and flow in some way go into the Blocked area at the bottom of the **In Progress** column. The team reviews the **Blocked** area every morning during standup to see if there's anything that can be done to get the task unblocked.

> ## SMILEY METRICS
>
> *Collect psycho-metrics to foster continuous improvement. Team demeanor directly relates to quality product, on-time performance, and degree of innovation possible.*

At the right edge of the board, is the **Check Automated Tests** column, which the team uses to track the daily task of monitoring the nightly automated tests. This column was added about a year into the transition to a pull-based board, specifically to cater for this daily recurring task.

This is a self-assigned task that generally happens first thing in the morning. The team member that takes on the task posts a summary, notifies development of new failures via e-mail or bug reports, and generates corresponding new task cards if work needs to be done by the Test team.

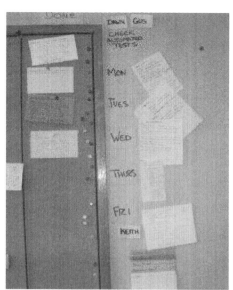

Process Overheads—Meetings and Metrics

Daily Standup Meeting
The team meets at 9:30am every morning in front of the kanban board to go over the **In Progress** and **Completed** task cards from the day before, prioritize work for the coming day, ensure that everyone's WIP is appropriate, and expedite resolution of blocked issues.

Sprint Planning Meeting While the team continues to have a weekly sprint, the weekly planning meeting evolved into the Monday morning standup. The team now simply spends a little extra time focusing on what they want to work on for the week and moves relevant task cards into the **Ready** column.

Monthly Planning Meeting Once a month, the XTest team meets with Development toprioritize the backlog in the **Input Queue** and to create new task cards based on feature workcurrently under development. This has greatly improved the visibility of upcoming work for the Test team, and helps to cement the ongoing communication between developers and testers.

Sprint Retrospectives Weekly retrospectives used to be held on Fridays, but were dissolved in December

BEYOND AGILE

2010 when the team became much smaller. The team is now able to more easily communicate needs for process improvements on an ongoing and as-needed basis during standups. Any actions required from retrospectives feed into the **Input Queue** and are prioritized along with other testing work.

CONTINUOUS IMPROVEMENT

Attachmate collected began with standard metrics and practices for software development. They used their visual systems to become comfortable with their work and optimize over time. This meant that as they learned, they discarded some metrics and meetings for others that simply worked better.

Metrics in Use The team is no longer estimating work or calculating metrics. Removing this administrative tracking overhead has enabled the team to focus on visualizing all of their work flows and regularly pull tasks through to meet the overall product release schedules, instead of trying to fit work into virtual time boxes. In addition, the visual evidence of progress provided by the **Done** column filling up every week is highly motivating.

Process Innovations Born out of Learning

*This task has been sitting in the Input Queue
for WAY too long!*

The **Planning/Analysis** column was added after about nine months in order to address task cards that had been sitting in the **Input Queue** for a long time. Often cards lingered because the task was too ambiguous or complex. Now, the person taking on a card is responsible for figuring out how to break down the work into doable tasks and return these tasks to the **Input Queue** (or directly to **Ready**). Items that go in this column may also just need additional evaluation about whether the task is worth doing at the time or whether its scope needs to be changed. It's acceptable for a task to sit in **Planning/Analysis** for over a week, but the goal is to get it moving again. As these tasks are actively discussed in standups, there is no risk of them stalling indeterminately.

*I thought **you** were going to check the test results!*

The **Automated Tests Tracking** section of the board was added to address two recurring issues, both resulting from the lack of clear communication between team members. The first was that team members who came into the office before the 9:30am Standup meeting were often eager to monitor the test results from the previous night. There were cases when multiple people were doing this task simultaneously. This duplication of work was identified as a waste. The second issue was that on some days nobody reviewed the test results, or perhaps only some of the results were reviewed.

As daily monitoring of the automated tests is a high priority responsibility for this team, they needed a way to make this work more visible and accountable. Writing a new task card each day felt wasteful. The solution was to create the **Check Automated Tests** column at the far right of the anban board. This provides a visual tracking mechanism to show that the job has been done, and the daily progression of test results are conveniently reflected in a central location where everybody can see the test failures and follow through on resolving broken tests.

PROCESS IS CONTEXTUAL

Attachmate continuously evolved their kanban board and team process according to emergent needs and context. There is no such thing as "ideal," only a board that serves the current situation, and serves it well. In this case, they are temporarily ramping up automated testing, so they temporarily altered the board to more effectively reflect reality.

If someone had reviewed the test results before the standup meeting then time is spent during the meeting to go over the findings and write new tasks if necessary. If nobody has yet self-assigned the task by then, the assignment is made during the meeting and test results are posted on the board during the day. The person who took on the task is then responsible for writing any necessary task cards to resolve any issues that come up.

OrganizationalExpansion of Kanban

The members of the XTest team have become cheerleaders at Attachmate, extolling the virtues of using Kanban through word of mouth and special presentations.

Although only a few groups outside of Test Engineering have adopted this approach, exciting signs of broader process evolution have started to emerge.

In May 2011, the XTest team expressed a need for better visibility into work being done by Development, so that feature work could flow through to Testing more smoothly. When the Test team came up with a utility that could easily print cards for tickets in their Extraview system, Development readily agreed to use a Kanban board to visualize their work. They found that having physical cards for their work has made it easier to group and prioritize their work.

The weekly Development and Testing status meetings, previously held in a conference room, have now been replaced with weekly standups in front of the Development board, with the odd visit to the XTest team board to clarify testing work. Meeting in front of the board has made conversations

> **FOCUS**
>
> *Having a visual aid to assist conversations makes communication much more effective. Meeting participants are working from a common understanding not only of the topic at hand, but also the context in which it is occurring.*

more focused. People are collaborating more effectively and they are better able to ensure that only the most important work is being completed at any given time.

In May 2011 the XTest team merged with another team in the Test Engineering group, adding more team members and increasing the WIP limit to three for all stages. As the other team was also using Kanban, the merger

BEYOND AGILE

was quite seamless. Several Personal Kanban[2] boards have popped up as well, as the positive effects of this tool have spread.

Remaining Challenges to Embrace

What, our solution isn't perfect?

An emerging question for the team is how to archive information. Right now, the team can't easily answer questions such as: *"So, how did we do a similar task before?" "Didn't we have a similar problem with this test system component in the past?" "Gosh, I wish we could go back in time to figure that out."* A searchable digital tracking system to mine this kind of information would be very helpful. But so far, the team has not completely switched to a digital system—mostly due to the additional overhead such a move would incur. The team also really likes the visibility and tangibility of a physical board and is afraid of losing that benefit by going digital.

> ### EXPERIMENT FIRST
>
> *The XTest team is more comfortable with the physical board, but they feel the need for deeper analytics and tracking. Their first experiment is with Cuanto, but they are treating it as an experiment – not overhauling their processes to suit a new potentially good idea. Based on the experiment, they may seek future process improvement.*

Some of the manual reporting has been replaced by moving the majority of the test results to a new open source test tracking and analysis tool called Cuanto, which allows testing notes to be added directly to the test result database.

---

2   *A specific interpretation of Kanban for use by individuals and small teams. See Benson and Barry, Personal Kanban(2011, Modus Cooperandi Press) for more details*

Keith, you're doing too much work at once again!

Maintaining a WIP of 2 has been somewhat challenging for some team members, since it is possible to physically assign yourself more than two tasks at time. If someone has a WIP of overt wo, it gets discussed during the morning standup meeting and the team helps this person prioritize his or her work. This may result in an item being returned to **Ready**, moved to **Blocked** or assigned to another person on the team.

One of the hardest things to figure out is what to do with a task that requires some wait time to determine if the task has been completed successfully. For example, let's say you have two task cards assigned to yourself. For one task, you need to investigate an automated functional test failure. The failure was determined to be due to a bug in the test system framework. You think you fixed this bug, but you want to wait until the next day after the tests run to confirm that the fix worked in the production environment.

> ## WIP
>
> *Work-in-Progress means different things to different types of work. It, too, is contextual. Find the WIP that works for your situation.*

So, while you wait, you work on another similar task that you fix and on which you again have to wait for confirmation. You're ready to move to a third task, but your WIP now exceeds two. Lately, the team has been experimenting with moving these tasks to **Blocked** while they wait. Technically, the **Blocked** column is for items that need to be addressed by someone outside of our team, so these tasks don't really fit, but it helps address going afoul of the WIP limit. Another option would be to tag the card in some way. For now, the **Blocked** approach is working well enough, since all blocked items are discussed daily in standups, ensuring that they do not fall beneath the radar.

So when does testing need to be complete for Service Pack 2?

Since no specific Sprints are defined, and the team is confined purely by product release schedules, the team has started talking about adding an additional visual that maps out product release milestones so that they can better prioritize work and develop backlog items based on release-related tasks.

Conclusions

Kanban is working well for the XTest team and the way the team works is continuously improving. Morale has improved through seeing tasks pulled more smoothly across the board to completion. The **Input Queue** is now only replenished when it's running low to prevent the team from feeling overwhelmed or doing a lot of early work in defining a task or project that may not be a priority when the time comes to work on it. The big key to their success is that they are now continuously listening to each other, constantly making suggestions for improvement, and trying out new ideas.

To quote Dawn Hemminger:

"Kanban works for us, because it best reflects how we actually work, instead of how we thought we should be working. The slow changes over time become seamless. We're doing our work more effectively without feeling forced to change with no reason."

AGILE AUTOMOTIVE

Building an Open Source Manufactory at WIKISPEED

Vital Statistics

Company: WIKISPEED
Location: Seattle, Washington State, United States
Industry and Domain:
Automobile manufacture
Insights by: Joe Justice

Joe Justice is an agile business process consultant and *"entreprenerd"* from the Seattle area. Since 2006, he's also a registered automotive manufacturer. In 2010, Joe's X Prize team, WIKISPEED, used agile processes to tie for 10th place in the mainstream class of the Progressive Insurance Automotive X Prize, a $10 million challenge for 100+ MPGe automobiles. WIKISPEED now continues to use agile processes to sell cars and rapidly solve

problems for social good. Joe has spoken on social web application development, project methodology, and agile best practices to audiences at Denver University, University of California Berkeley, Google, The Bill and Melinda Gates Foundation, Rotary International, and others. Joe is a nominated TEDx speaker and currently a business process consultant at SolutionsIQ and CEO of WIKISPEED.

INTRODUCTION

WIKISPEED is a licensed automotive manufacturing company, building road legal 100+ mpg commuter cars that most car companies might dream to have in their portfolios. The company competes in a highly regulated industry, has no paid staff, and is run solely by volunteers distributed over twenty countries.

Their first product is the SGT01 (Super Grand Touring 01); a 100 mile-per-gallon, four-seat commuter car using a mid-engine and rear-wheel drive layout, designed for efficiency of power delivery and balance in all weather conditions. Their goal is to mass produce this vehicle with a target price of $17,995, and as of this writing they sell prototypes to the public for $25,000 to finance their R&D.

With only a few volunteers dedicated full-time to commercialize this car and most volunteers operate out of spare bedrooms or home garages. WIKISPEED leverages Agile, Lean, Scrum, and Kanban to make products aimed at revolutionizing the industry itself.

WIKISPEED's bootstrapped nature and single product means that they enjoy considerable product focus. This means that while traditional automotive manufacturing relies on development cycles of 3 to 25 years, WIKISPEED retools their car every 7 days.

WIKISPEED IN INCUBATION

Joe Justice was one of those college kids swept up in the Fast and Furious sport compact car renaissance in the early 2000s; where lightness, nimble handling and efficiency mattered more than fuel spent chasing peak torque. When Joe graduated from the University of Wyoming with a Bachelor's in Computer Science and he went to work for an Agile software development company and then moved on to Agile consulting projects. Joe had a passion for efficiency, not just in software development, but also in cars. He was fascinated by the science behind how the new crop of tiny sports cars was achieving higher safety scores and faster race track times than the bigger, more expensive, fuel-swilling V8s.

What was merely curiosity became a serious project when Joe realized that taking more weight out of his Honda without compromising safety would mean designing his own chassis, or frame, for the car. In 2006 he registered himself as a legal automotive manufacturer and proto-typed two lightweight chassis that were close to legal specifications. In 2008 the Progress Insurance X Prize Competition was announced, offering $10 million to the car that could best perform at 100 miles per gallon (mpg) and meet road legal safety specifications.

Joe spent three months writing a software program to simulate the per-second fuel consumption of vehicles and verified it against the mile-per-gallon test results of commercial cars. His computer program estimated that his prototype chassis, if finished, would achieve 70 mpg EPA. This meant that Joe had a fighting chance at winning the X Prize[1]. After long, heart-to-heart discussions with his wife and careful planning together, they broke the piggy bank, taking all their savings to pay for the $5,000.00 USD entrance fee to the X Prize Competition.

THE HOBBY GETS SERIOUS

Now fully vested and committed to building a 100 mpg car that meets road legal specifications, Joe found himself at a serious disadvantage. Up against teams from global companies like Tata and Tesla, and top notch schools such as Massachusetts Institute of Technology (MIT), all with millions of dollars of funding behind them, his tinkering alone in a Denver garage did not instill confidence.

> **INTRINSIC MOTIVATION**
>
> *Tapping into intrinsic motivation creates teams dedicated to creating a product.*

This is where the story takes its first unconventional swerve. He took an approach similar to writing open source software—that is, he made his objectives and his work progress as visible to the public as possible.

He created a blog, sharing his experiences: what went well, what didn't go well, and what he might try next. He asked basic and complicated questions to the world

---

1   *http://progressiveautoxprize.org*

at large. Soon, people were not only commenting on his blog and answering tough questions, but they actually stopped by Joe's garage to take a look at what was going on. Then people started staying to help.

Realizing what was happening, Joe found the main ingredient that would enable him to compete against the well-funded teams: *Enthusiasm*. A team was never part of Joe's original vision, but his Agile project management experience from his software consulting day-job enabled him to take advantage of things that show up at his doorstep.

On April 9th 2010, the WIKISPEED car passed every technical requirement for the X Prize contest and became one of 36 global finalists heading to the track at Michigan International Speedway, from an original field of 136 cars.

Soon, WIKISPEED was 12 cars away from winning first place in the Mainstream Class. This was a critical moment for Joe and his family. He and his wife made the call to take what was meant to be a down payment for a home in Seattle and bought the parts and materials instead to build the version of the car that would campaign in the X Prize events. Additionally, they brought in donations via the team's website, ranging from $1 all the way up to $35,000, all collected via PayPal. At this point, WIKISPEED hummed with 44 committed team members from four different countries.

How did WIKISPEED design and manufacture a car out of Joe's home garage based on volunteer help and donations? What gave them the courage to compete head to head against Tata, Tesla, and MIT, all backed by heavy-weight investors? The answer lies in continuous process improvement and rapid iterative development.

Evolution #1: Modularization

With development of the car happening in multiple locations, WIKISPEED needed a strategy that would allow for parallel development without introducing potential conflict between different components being built simultaneously. The team needed to reduce the cost to make frequent changes to the car, so they could afford hundreds of iterations to get the car just right.

Software teams have been coping with this problem for years, and have found an elegant answer in "contract first development." This means designing how objects connect—their "interface"—before designing the objects themselves.

At WIKISPEED, that answer led them to first design how parts of the car would connect structurally, how they would communicate information like wheel speed and fuel level, and then to design those parts. Any part built to that contractual interface, would work with all the other parts that met that contract, whether they were built in Ireland or South Africa, or designed 18 months ago or 20 minutes ago.

In practice, this meant designing a chassis with contract mountings, with all subsequently built components being modularized to bolt on to the mountings. The only dependency for those components would be the contract to the chassis itself, eliminating any dependencies across components or even to a particular version of the chassis. The chassis would then act as a frame, the skeletal architecture of the car, while all other components, such as the suspension, brake system and engine module, are attached to the skeletal framework. This way unforeseen costs resulting from changes downstream would be minimized. Individual components, or modules, could evolve independently of each other without fear of redundancy and rework, thereby saving time, money, and more importantly, ensuring forward momentum in this ad hoc distributed team.

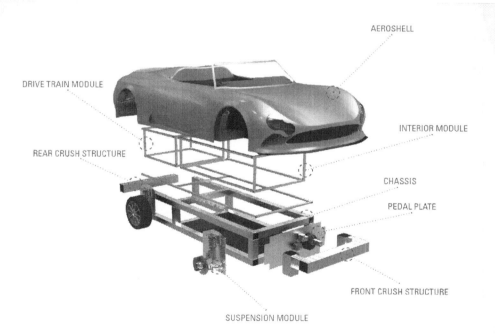

Examples of Modularized Components

The chassis is agnostic to the type of suspension the car accommodates. This means the team can try any new suspension setup they can come up with, or even wings or skis, in about the time it takes to change a tire. This lets them move quickly and makes radical changes not only possible, but inexpensive and easy to apply.

⇨   The engine and entire power train can be swapped out equally rapidly. In fact, the car is designed in such a way that it can make use of any engine technology without changing other parts of the car or without a long development cycle; be it a gasoline, diesel, bio-diesel, or an electric engine. This lets the team test one engine on a test bench while another engine is in the car completing test laps, pull the car in, switch the two engines, and continue testing.

⇨   The braking system is part of the pedal plate module. Any new brake design that

> ## LOOSELY COUPLED
>
> *WIKISPEED's modular physical design is echoed by the distributed team members. They all have clear means of interfacing with the rest of the team. The clarity of the product, which is maintained by short deployment cycles and visual controls, allows the staff to be modular as well. There is not enough time to become lost.*

fits on that plate can be tested quickly. Team members can experiment with a wide array of braking technologies without having to make changes to any of the other modules.

This strategy was one of WIKISPEED's strongest advantages compared to their X Prize competitors. They were able to easily adopt any new technology hot from the laboratory or the open market, with minimal costs and minimal changes.

Thanks to this modular design, WIKISPEED avoided extra work that resulted from new improvements and could implement them right away. This saved them time, effort, and materials, all of which WIKISPEED used sparingly because they had very little of them.

While consumers may appreciate that the chassis and modules are built for 5-star crash rating equivalency, the true beauty of this chassis module can only be appreciated by those who constantly invent better components for the car.

Evolution #2: Absorbing More Team Members

With all the publicity given to the project, WIKISPEED has attracted experts from a range of industries—from materials science to aerodynamics to facility management and flow-based manufacturing—all sharing skills and learning new ones. With over 150 volunteers across 15 countries, many work out of their own spare bedrooms, storage units, and garages, then send the prototyped parts to Seattle, where each part is tested.

However, WIKISPEED had to figure out how to responsibly work with all types of people whenever they had time to contribute, from whatever distributed location they happened to be in. Typical employers worry that a new team member may take more time being trained than they can contribute. Training, for WIKISPEED simply wasn't possible. Deployment was happening too

BEYOND AGILE

quickly, and many team members were only working on the project for weeks, days, or even hours.

The solution goes back to apprenticeship in the middle ages and even earlier, and has been accelerated and streamlined by extreme programming (XP). "Pairing" is a technique where an experienced team member pairs up with someone who is excited about a particular task, but hasn't actually done it before. At the end of the task, two people know how to do it.

This organically scales knowledge out through the team, shares specialized skills, and builds a cross-functional team without any time dedicated to train- ing and minimal time spent on documenting methods. By pairing individuals with one another to get work done, they cross-train each other, and every team member becomes multi-functional.

> ## SCALING EFFECTIVELY
>
> *WIKISPEED does not have the luxury of training or even an on-boarding process. With a combination of pairing and directed training, new team members can quickly get to work.*

With minimal effort and zero time and resources dedi- cated specifically to training, WIKISPEED manages to elevate the overall skill level of the entire distributed team.

A case in point that illustrates how well this approach works, is the involvement of Rob Mohrbacher. Rob Mohrbacher is an expert in composites. His day job involves designing large-scale unmanned, remote control and autonomous aircraft in Germantown, Maryland. When WIKISPEED came to Mohrbacher's attention, he got right to work designing the new body for the car, and shared his design iterations regularly to let the team "remote pair" and learn the methods. Mohrbacher emailed a portfolio of designs to the team. The team collaboratively worked with Mohrbacher to develop the body module the team would build next. This car body turned out to be one of Mohrbacher's most widely known works, and WIKISPEED built it into the car while learning some of Mohrbacher's methods and crediting him, before ever having met the man in person.

Evolution #3: The Team Process That Made Ultra Distributed Collaboration Possible

How is it possible that Mohrbacher, who is geographically isolated from the rest of the team and has never even seen the prototype of the car, manages to create numerous viable, aerodynamically compatible car body designs? The answer lies in a flexible system of communication—both verbal and electronic.

Communication. Every week on Thursday at 6pm Seattle time, everyone local meets at the nearest WIKISPEED shop. Joe heads in to the one located at the north end of Seattle. All available team members dial in via Skype or FreeConferenceCall.com to join the weekly standup. At this standup, they each describe what they accomplished in the last week and any blocked tasks. Then they share a demo of the current state of the project, often through a YouTube video, and finally commit to tasks that each team member will take on during the next week. Since most people work on WIKISPEED tasks throughout the week, daily progress is also communicated via email sent through a Google Groups distribution list. That is, seven people could have made progress at seven distinct times of the week, and everyone is privy to a practically real-time update on any progress made. In addition to these daily emails, team members also actively post pictures of recent progress on Facebook on the WIKISPEED Facebook page.

> **TOOLS**
>
> *Business loves tools. Buying a tool feels like an investment in the future. However, just like process is contextual, so too are tools. Choose tools carefully and only after you adequately understand what the tool will do for you and what you really need.*

The team makes use of social media, like Facebook, YouTube, and Twitter. Facebook serves as a duplicate of workflow documentation, providing a detailed history of what was done at any given time. Secondly, this provides the public with an open and transparent view of the state of development at WIKISPEED. If anyone wants to make a donation or contribute help and knowledge, they have a real-time update on what they are paying for, and insight into the people with whom they will work.

In other words, stakeholders are privy to all the information that team members have, and any line between being interested, being a stakeholder, and becoming a team member is light and easy to cross. Since many stakeholders are customers and many team members are stakeholders, dissolving information barriers between these groups made it even easier for the interested public to become involved.

The added advantage of using public social media services for communication is that there is also less need to allocate resources towards customer and donor relations. The project updates pretty much take care of all of that. Since many team members use LinkedIn, this also allows the team to get to know all the team members better without filling in internal employee profiles or HR site information like a traditional company might request. WIKISPEED reduces process overhead by going to where the people are already sharing information and joining the party.

Sprint Planning. By virtue of the nature of research and development, the WIKISPEED team was not operating from a rigid central plan. WIKISPEED is in a discovery phase and therefore actively avoids planning any work beyond two weeks out. Longer planning periods quickly become obsolete for the team. In fact, sprint planning is more about maximizing the amount of planning avoided. This is because the team, materials, machinery, and even goals are continually changing, so most time spent planning would be waste. For one, the X-Prize committee changed the terrain of the race several times during the competition timeline. This meant that many other teams had to build entire new cars to remain competitive. For the WIKISPEED team, this simply meant re-focusing all their energy to rapidly develop new modules.

Staying flexible and easily adaptable translates into making progress without narrowing down future options, as honed in "real option theory" project management. An example of this is the concept of stubs. When looking at a project as big as building a car, it's easily to be paralyzed by the daunting size of the work. Where to start? It can feel difficult to proceed on any one part of the car without knowing all the details of its neighboring parts.

This is where the stub comes in. You do just enough work to define the maximum likely parameters of the parts next to the part you know the most about, and then you mock up that part in cheap material. For example, the first version of the suspension module was a stub made of wood blocks that bolted onto the chassis suspension contracts and held the car at the 4," speed bump clearing, regulation ride height. That let work proceed on the engine system and interior. Having broken down a major component into smaller pieces defined by stubs, small steps made progress visible, and team members were quickly high-fiving each other before a full suspension was even built. The first parking brake handle was a cardboard box as big as the largest parking brake handle they were likely to use, letting the team work on the nearby steering wheel and seat mounts with confidence of placement.

However, there is still some planning and organization that WIKISPEED must do. They keep a prioritized backlog of enough work to deliver the next major customer-visible value. They utilize Google Docs, DropBox, and SkyDrive as cloud stores of versioned documents, and contributions flag their work in the kanban backlog as **Pending Review**, **In Progress**, and **Done**, along with any comments attached. The team shares grant applications, contracts, investor letters, architecture and diagrams, software code for embedded systems in the car and the website, and CAD files. Physical parts are mailed through FedEx, USPS, UPS, or hand-delivered by enthusiastic team members excited to make a road trip and meet the team members they have been remotely pairing with over Skype and the phone.

The Kanban: WIKISPEED constantly tinkers to build processes that don't require a lot of explanation to new team members so they can sustain their constant, high workflow. This has a lot to do with how they utilized their kanban.

In the beginning, WIKISPEED planned and documented their workflow in a plain text file with an ordered list of things to do. With more team members joining, this list soon became a series of calendar invites to attach work time blocks to ordered tasks. To help with visualizing the big picture, those tasks were printed out and tacked up on the wall in the main shop. These printouts eventually turned into sticky notes on a big piece of white cardboard tacked up on the wall, letting team members re-prioritize work without printing new sheets. At this point, there were remote team members but the majority of the team was co-located in Seattle. This enabled the whole team to visualize the workflow, which was a big moment for many team members as they saw more of the bigger picture and the rate of work (throughput).

Eventually, team members donated whiteboards, where they drew swimlanes and columns for the sticky notes, which allowed them to change or improve columns regularly and swimlanes as needed. This allowed the team to modify their process more rapidly as the team grew. The WIKISPEED team attempted to use online, digital backlogs, but these online tools were too regimented, and took away the free-form placement of sticky notes.

To accommodate the geographic diversity of the team, and as the team grew larger, WIKISPEED eventually established sub-teams based on the type of work. Some of these sub-teams successfully maintained and utilized online backlogs, but they ran into difficulties when communicating work progress with the larger team. Then the WIKISPEED team found Scrumy. Scrumy doesn't have much flexibility or allow teams to explicitly limit their Work-in-Progress, but Joe found it intuitive for new team members to use without any training. Sub-teams could now easily share information with the main team, or move between teams easily without losing track of progress.

How Does the Team Maintain Workflow?

Having a kanban board that explains the entire process without any training is central to maintaining a smooth workflow in the team. This enables the team to reorganize without losing touch with other parts of the team. This also gives the team's ScrumMaster enough information to help people limit their Work-in-Process (WIP) and apply other optimizations to increase flow.

To get things done as effectively as possible, the team also reorganizes as needed. People can switch to work on vastly different parts of the project and see where in the organization their skills are needed or where there is something exciting for them to learn. Team members constantly align with each other to pair and group to work on the prioritized tasks.

Thanks to modularization and stubs, these pairs can make parallel changes without ever stepping on each other's toes. Modularization removes any potential for the team to block each other internally. If there are external forces at play that present an obstacle, the team members "swarm" around the pair facing the problem, and collectively solve the problem. *How do team members sense that someone needs extra help?* Even new team members notice body language and tone of voice changes from a pair that has just come up against a blocking issue. This is one of the reasons the shop in Seattle is designed to be as audio-visually open as possible. If a pair suddenly becomes very quiet, or someone starts slumping their shoulders, or if someone starts re-organizing the whole toolbox, that is an implicit call for help. The team members are very keen on looking out for each other, because they all have one common goal—to build the most awesome car ever.

Onboarding New Team Members in 5 Minutes

The team process has to be rigorous enough to build products that comply with NHTSA, IIHS, and FMVSS (motor industry) regulations. And the process has to be lightweight enough for new team members to use it with a minimum of training. WIKISPEED has encapsulated the methodology, enough to get started, into a 5-minute orientation. Entering one of the WIKISPEED shops, after being welcomed, you might be offered an orientation like this:

"The safety shelf is on your left, all safety gear is there. If you find safety gear out that isn't being used, please put it back on that shelf. Each time you start a task, look at the safety shelf and borrow everything you might be able to use." Then,

"The snack shelf is next to the safety shelf, it is just as important. All snacks are donated, they are here for you, so use them."

Now looking out at the color-coded shelves stacked with matching color-coded transparent bins: "The white shelf has transparent bins of all of our hand power tools. If you don't see something you need, donate it to us and find something we do have that will work in the meantime. The yellow shelf is all of our manual hand tools." And now to the process:

"This is our kanban. Take a sticky note as close to the top left of the **Backlog** *column as you can, that is either exciting to you or you already know how to do it. Put it in the* **In Progress** *col-*

umn. Then shout to the shop the name of the task you just took, and ask who here knows the most about it, and who wants to pair with you. Write your name and your pair name down on the kanban next to your sticky note, then listen to what the most knowledgeable person about that task has to say about it. When you think you are done, move your card to the **Pending Review** *column and shout to the shop the name of the task and that you think you are done. Someone will come over, inspect the work, and either move your task to* **Done** *or will create a new task of what needs to be completed for that task to be done."*

That's safety orientation, tool orientation, and process documentation—in 5 minutes.

The kanban tells the team what needs to be done next in priority order, who is doing what now, what is pending review, and what was done so far this week. The quality bar is built in through the Subject Matter Expert (SME) task launch and review, and knowledge-sharing is built in through pairing. Provided the Product Owner keeps a clear vision of the end state and prioritizes the backlog regularly, this is the entire process for running the shop.

Is it Scrum or is it Kanban?

Team WIKISPEED uses the three Scrum roles: Product Owner, ScrumMaster, and Team. Team WIKISPEED also conducts three of the four Scrum ceremonies: stand-ups, demos and retrospectives.

One Scrum ritual, sprint planning, is usually skipped by the team. The kanban holds the team's backlog and allows them to accept new work through a real-time real-options assessment. This allows the WIKISPEED team to experience the benefits of flow, while still holding on to some Scrum structure.

> **SCRUMBAN**
>
> *The term "Scrumban" has erroneously been used to refer to a hybrid of Scrum and Kanban. This portmanteau term was originally coined by Corey Ladas as a metaphor for an evolution from time-boxed agile development (Scrum) to continuous flow (Kanban), not a hybrid of the two approaches. See in that light, WIKISPEED has built its foundation on flow, and uses some Scrum practices to facilitate team efficiency and planning.*

The team also does not estimate work unless they have a specific timed opportunity, like a car show or a racing event, and even then they simply bring the most up to date car they have instead of setting arbitrary goals that may lead to an unsustainable work pace or a drop in quality.

A Highly Regulated Industry

The team products have to meet some very stringent and often frequently evolving US Federal regulations. This is a context which has in the past often been thought as a poor fit for Agile methods, however it was the birthplace of Lean. Kanban as a flow-based system, allowed the WIKISPEED team to leverage some Agile innovations as well.

For example, each regulation had pass and fail criteria. It was therefore easy to turn each regulation into a test, and use Agile's concept of Test-Driven Development (TDD).

By starting with a failing test and building to pass that test, work can be easily focused on passing a specific test. After regulations are met, market differentiators and ever increasing customer-visible value are phrased in testable stories to be iterated through via TDD. As regulations change, tests adapt to pass the new context.

Tests as Success Criteria

In geometry, we know that the shortest distance between two points is a straight line. In Lean, this translates to focus on where you are, where you want to be, and the shortest practical road to get there. Forget all other distractions.

WIKISPEED focus on tests as their only success criteria, and never keep metrics that do not directly relate to winning the X Prize or making

> **MEASURES OF SUCCESS**
>
> *Success criteria for WIKISPEED relate directly to tangible delivered value. Derivative measures, like velocity shown in Scrum's burndown charts or Kanban's cycle time shown in cumulative flow diagrams, should always be secondary measures to actual delivery.*

safe, ultra-efficient cars. Examples for success criteria in test-driven manufacturing are, *"this bolt needs to support 8,000 lbs of lateral force before failure"* or *"the turn signal cannot have a delay of over x milliseconds"* or *"I can stow 20 grocery bags in the trunk and a laptop in the glove-box."* This helps keep the project focused on real outcomes and avoids any work that isn't focused on making a failing test, or unmet success criteria, pass.

Measuring the right success criteria also boosts team morale, because everyone can see exactly how passing a test directly impacts their likelihood of winning the race. It's easy to understand the project scope when looking at a wall of red lights, and it's easy to boost morale when a failing test red light turns into a bright green light; everybody claps or high-fives and throughput goes up.

Team Morale

Joe is a strong proponent of team morale. In his own words, "morale is a multiplier for velocity." To him, frustration is creativity's worse enemy and any time not spent creatively solving problems is best avoided. The team looks at the flow of the work, using value stream maps, to avoid any time not creatively solving problems. The value stream map itself isn't creatively solving problems, so they map quickly to get just enough information to identify any bottlenecks and add tasks to the backlog to try to remove them. Then it's back to solving problems, because WIKISPEED observes the biggest morale booster in a project is regular success visible across an open, collaborative work area.

Not Winning the X Prize

For a brief few days, the team had a 1-in-10 shot at the $5 million dollar prize purse

THE VICTORY OF DEFEAT

The WIKISPEED team probably wouldn't have come along as fast and as far as they had (or even believed it was possible!) if they hadn't had the original tangible goal post of winning the X Prize competition. The competition deadline set very clear criteria for a shippable Version 1 of their product. Not winning the competition, left them with tangible market feedback they could use to improve Version 2.

allocated to the Mainstream Class winner-take-all 1st place finisher. However, the team eventually tied for 10th and, as you can imagine, hit a definite low point. That lasted for about one hour. Then they were buzzing again—*"We tied for 10th place in the X Prize!"* Quickly team members made plans to implement what they had learned during the events, updated the backlog, and re-committed time to research and build.

When they started out, WIKISPEED was aiming to win the X Prize. Little did they know then that this design would be one that could make it to the consumer market. In January 2011, the team brought the evolved car to the largest auto show in the world, where they were invited to show their public sale production prototype on the main floor between Ford and Chevrolet. That car was featured by Automobile Magazine, the Discovery Channel, and press in every United Nations language. WIKISPEED continues to evolve the car to reduce complexity and increase efficiency while maintaining safety, with the goal of bringing these cars to market with triple the efficiency of existing economy commuter cars and the same, or lower, total cost of ownership.

The Real Prize: The Open Source Car as the New Business Model

The WIKISPEED team aims to grow by continuously creating visible customer value. They have one goal: build a fuel-efficient car that their customers will love and will keep them safe. What do customers love, apart from the car itself?

As a volunteer-driven, donation-based closed corporation without a profit motive, WIKISPEED doesn't just create value for customers, it also values the involvement of people. A volunteer could one day become a customer. A donor could also pre-order a car. The team values the input of these people. They listen to their feedback, and try to incorporate the feedback into the car. Customers can also become team members and contribute as much or as little as they would like.

The WIKISPEED development model and organizational structure are somewhat similar to those of open source software groups. The well-known open source operating system Linux didn't become a leading platform in its industry because someone had the perfect vision in mind and built it all alone. On the contrary, Linux gained traction because Linus Torvalds initiated the development of Linux and allowed anyone who knew anything about the operating system to improve it. Linus understood that users are the first people to find faults in the software. He also realized that impatient users would be willing to help fix bugs in exchange for a better version of the software. It was a win-win situation. The only drawback was that Linus couldn't claim all the glory.

Ironically, he was given credit for something much larger than just the software itself: the concept of open source software. Can WIKISPEED do the same and build a superior vehicle to those produced by the proprietary models in the automotive industry?

Continuously Deploying a Car

Continuous development, visualized through their kanban, allows WIKISPEED to maximize customer benefits. Their concept is this: an existing owner of a WIKISPEED car can upgrade to the latest model at any point in time without having to pay the full price of a new car. The car is composed of 8 modules that are continually undergoing improvements in 7-day cycles. A customer can purchase only the component they're interested in.

For example, WIKISPEED has plans to produce upgrades for existing owners, such as a warm leather winter edition interior module and a cool wicker summer edition picnic interior. The team is also developing a module that can switch cars that are on the road now from gasoline to electric or to bio-diesel fuel. This allows customers to have a closer purchasing relationship with the company and provides a tighter feedback loop to team members.

New customers, instead of waiting for next year's model, always get the latest and greatest that is available the week their car is built.

GOOD MIGRATIONS
Getty Images Scrumban Marathon

VITAL STATISTICS

Company: *Getty Images*
Location: *Seattle, Washington State, United States*
Industry and Domain: *Media*
Insights by: *Jeff Oberlander*

Jeff is currently the Vice President of Engineering at Navigating Cancer in Seattle, Washington. At the time of this story, he was the Senior Director of Application Development at Getty Images. He has over 20 years of professional software leadership, development, design, and architecture experience at both large and small companies throughout the American Northwest. Jeff is an expert practitioner, coach, trainer, and mentor in Lean and Agile principles and practices, working as a developer on XP teams, transforming teams to Scrum, and working as an enterprise Lean-Agile coach.

INTRODUCTION

In 2005, Getty Images was building their software using traditional waterfall practices. At the time, they were generating over US$500 million in annual revenue, most of which flowed directly through their e-commerce website. The site was seeing 11 million unique visitors per month, delivering over 10 million images, and handling 6 million searches per day. This hugely popular site was a 24-7 global cash register for Getty Images and any site downtime affected revenue instantly.

The Getty Images customer base included major advertising agencies and companies across the world, as well as heavy photo users like Sports Illustrated, People Magazine, Time-Life, and nearly all American morning newspapers. Content delivery had to respond as fast as new worldwide events occurred. Time to market of new features was critical.

Despite the fact that Getty Images had built a booming e-commerce business between 1995-2005, the company found itself with a technology platform that had accumulated a significant amount of technical debt, making it difficult to support further business growth. The development process as well as the underlying code and technology platform were all creating delays in bringing enhancements to market. Simply put, the business had outgrown its current processes and technology. Changes were needed on many fronts if Getty Images were to remain as successful as before.

In August 2005, Getty Images duly embarked on the ambitious task of rebuilding its primary website and all of its primary back-end processing systems from the ground up. This included the image ingestion process, controlled vocabulary for tagging images, and the image search engine. (Nothing much really, just the heart of the entire web site.) It almost goes without saying that this was a critical undertaking for the company, both technically and operationally, and most certainly strategically.

As is often the case with such critical undertakings, there were a few hiccups along the way...

The "Web Vision" project, as it was dubbed, included over 20 project teams and over 150 people, including operations. The project ran for more than two years—a year longer than originally planned. When the new site was eventually delivered, its performance was terrible. It was extremely slow from the end-user perspective and many of the features did not make sense to them, leaving Getty Images with a slew of upset and frustrated customers.

This created the risk of losing both new and existing customers to competing sites. For the following four months, Getty Images found themselves fixing problems, unable to add any enhancements to the site that could deliver business value.

As high-profile and important as the site was to Getty Images, the executive team simply had to find a better way to do things. They could not continue to place their revenue stream at risk by continuing to develop and maintain the *gettyimages.com* site using processes and technology that were patently not working for them. They had to step out of their comfort zone—and quick.

In search of better answers, the leadership team attended a Lean-Agile Conference for the first time in January 2008. Enthused by what they saw and learnt, they came back to Getty Images committed to bringing Lean-Agile thinking into the Waterfall world of Getty Images. This is the story of their journey—of how they rolled out Scrum and subsequently Kanban across their entire enterprise of over 25 teams and 200 people, and the lessons they learnt along the way.

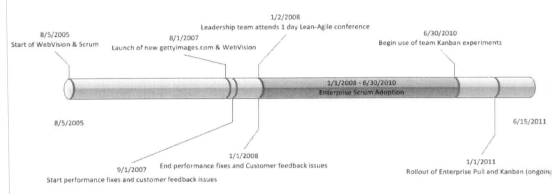

THE FRYING PAN AND THE FIRE

In 2005, the Getty Images web site was under severe strain, seriously affecting both business value and work conditions. Clients and stakeholders could not get new features into the system in time to meet the changing demands of their customers or the market. Production bugs were at an all-time high and software releases took weeks to stabilize both before and after launch.

Production support costs were sky-rocketing. The technical teams were spending long nights and weekends at the office trying to resolve the myriad of issues.

The development teams in particular were bearing a large measure of the pain. With deadlines looming, they regularly endured working late into the night, only to discover breaking issues in the final hour that caused management to hold off on the release altogether. Moreover, after a release, the development team had no insight into customer satisfaction. There was no feature feedback from either customers or stakeholders during development cycles in this period. For the development teams, this was like shooting blindfolded.

Planning for development also involved a considerable amount of wasted effort. Development work was planned using micro-estimation down to the hour by team leads or managers. These estimates were widely inaccurate, and served little purpose. Product owners would write extensive use case scenario documents that didn't help developers do their work. And on top of that, people were organized in silos according to organizational structure or specialization, creating an unnecessary communication barrier between functional teams when collaborating on a single feature.

In this environment, everyone felt like they were failing. The business could not get the work they needed from IT to meet the demands of the business, and the development and technology services teams worked long hours only to end up with frustrated and unhappy business stakeholders.

Delivery of Requirements

With the way things were at Getty Images, a business owner who wanted features that might take 3-4 days to develop would have to wait a minimum of 3 months to see it materialize on the website. This is because software releases were scheduled every 2 months and requirements had to be defined 1 month before the release cycle. In effect, this resulted in any feature—regardless of priority, size, or business value—having a minimum of 3 months lead time to market. In theory, that is.

> **MORALE HOLE**
>
> *Note how Jeff says "everyone felt like they were failing" and that "everyone" means developers, managers, literally everyone. The team felt their work wasn't good enough. The business felt it wasn't keeping up with market needs. Managers felt stuck in the middle. This low morale frustrated the entire organization.*

Typically, it was much longer because teams first had to plan which features would hit the requirements definition cycle first. Throughout this timeline, requirements would change, features would be moved in and out of releases, and time-to-market continued to stretch while business owners were spending time on wasteful work, creating feature inventories. In reality, time-to-market was 6 months or more in most cases. This was incredibly demoralizing for staff.

Organizational Structure

Across this 200+ IT department, the organization was structured as follows:

Tech Services (traditional operations group), Project Management Office (PMO), Quality Assurance (QA) and Application Development. Each of these areas had its own Vice President (VP). The PMO and QA oddly were organized under the same VP, but separated from development. The developers were organized under multiple directors around their own specialties, and never really cross-pollinated across those specialties. Not a single team was cross-functional.

Handoffs and Dependencies

Within this organizational structure, cross-team dependencies often affected productivity adversely. In the typical lifecycle of a feature, Project Managers (PMs), started by writing requirements for a feature. Then lead developers would write

> **MALEVOLENT PROCESS**
>
> *The hidden opportunity cost reflected in this convoluted requirements cycle is staggering. It goes beyond demoralizing your staff. This is business value being held ransom by inefficient process. The process itself creates additional waste making a self-perpetuating cycle geared against release of quality product.*

application architecture documents for the features, developers would implement the features, after which it was finally handed off to QA for testing. Once a feature entered the testing stage, developers and testers iteratively passed the feature back and forth to each other, each time making minimal effort to address each other's needs. Bug tracking systems abounded. Issues bounced from one team to the next, and all teams struggled to achieve the ever-elusive Zero Bug Bounce (ZBB) and Zero Resolved Bugs (ZRB) statuses before a release. The last person holding the bug felt the wrath of the VPs looking at open bug lists before the drop-dead date on release windows.

Broken process leading to low morale and productivity

Given the nature of requirements flow and change, coupled with a waterfall process that relied on strict deadlines and handoffs, and the siloed and specialized nature of teams, very little business value was being delivered, yet there was high cost to the business. Simply put, the Information Technology (IT) organization was unable to effectively meet the demands of Getty Images' digital media business in the time required by this very competitive market. The staff in Getty Images IT always felt busy and overworked and that they were failing to satisfy their business stakeholders.

INFANCY OF TRANSITION

An unofficial Scrum team in a Waterfall world

In 2005, Jeff was in charge of the Search team which was tasked to rebuild the company's search engine for the new Web Vision project. Before joining Getty Images, he had spent the previous 5 years adopting and leading Agile practices in other companies. Upon arriving at Getty Images, Jeff transitioned his team to Scrum, making it the only Agile team in a Waterfall organization. This Scrum setup had a virtual cross-functional team that included developers, testers, and a project manager. He worked with the project manager to establish a small product backlog, and then worked with the team to establish a sprint. The team set a technical goal for their first sprint, and proceeded each day with daily Scrums. At the end of the first sprint, Jeff conducted a sprint review for the business stakeholders, the Project Management Office group, and many others from the technology management team. People were thrilled to see the makings of the new search engine live only one month into the start of the project. This was the beginning of the first cross-functional and agile team at Getty Images.

The search team continued to adopt and ingrain this process for themselves over the next two years. At first, they had four-week sprints and monthly demos. The demos were not only about delivering requirements, but also focused on improving stakeholders' visibility into the team process. The team could not influence the process of planning releases, nor could they change any deadlines or requirements, but they changed the development process within their team, as that was something they could actually influence.

> **FAST CHANGE SHOCKS SYSTEMS**
>
> *Process adoptions often fail due to attempts to "drive change" rather than nurturing it to grow organically. Slower, more deliberate change tends to be more stable because more people involved understand why change is occurring and what specific changes are hoped to provide.*

They employed every Scrum tactic and tool. The team had its own product backlog, burndown charts, daily Scrums, and retrospectives. To create the new product backlog, the project manager wrote up stories based on material she pulled out of the larger out-of-date requirements documents.

> ## MORALE BOOST
>
> *It is also deeply motivating for the people doing the work to be given the opportunity to deliver achievable, measurable tasks that, when seen together, combine to form an important whole.*

Over time, other development teams started participating in the Search Team demo and sprint reviews. The demos were increasingly frequented by new teams, as well as their accompanying stakeholders, including executive management, program managers, and anyone interested in visibility into what was happening in development (which was most people).

As the demos became more popular, the Search Team developed a reputation for its productivity and predictability—delivering sprints of work month after month reliably. Since this was new development which would eventually launch a new website, the sprints were building up to the final product which would, when complete, flip all customers from the old web site to the brand new one. Compared to many of the other teams, the Search team's ongoing success month after month was extremely refreshing for the company. Their performance started receiving a lot of attention from the executive leadership, enabling Jeff to hire another agile development manager.

This manager also converted his team to Scrum, and they too showed an incredible productivity improvement in a very short timeframe.

Scrum and Agile were starting to catch on in Getty Images.

MASS TRANSITION

After investing two extremely long and arduous years, only to be hammered repeatedly by poor customer experience, the executive team was finally ready for some big process changes. In January 2008, Jeff organized a leadership outing to a free one-day Lean-Agile overview workshop in Seattle. The SVP of Technology, SVP of E-commerce, and several VP's, PM's and Getty Images management staff attended. The principles discussed were very enthusiastically received by the entire group. Given that there were proven success stories within Getty Images at this time, a decision was made to convert the whole development organization to Scrum and focus on Agile principles as an organization.

The question on the table was how? While converting one team at a time was a nice safe concept, the reality was that—given all of the dependencies between teams and Getty Images' tightly coupled release system—everyone really had to make the jump at the same time. Fortunately, by this time, there were several grass roots agile advocates and leaders appearing on the floor—developers, project managers and Product Owners. Jeff also had agile partners in the PMO, who were very enthusiastic advocates

and coaches within their own group. So even though the
IT organization was still siloed, the leadership/coaching
partnership between IT and the PMO really set the stage
for success.

Collapsing Teams

The first order of business was to create independent,
cross-functional teams. This change meant that there
would no longer be a separate Quality Assurance group
in the organization. All teams would henceforth consist
of both developers and testers under a single manager.
Each team was given full vertical ownership of a particular product.

Product Owners and Backlogs

The next step was redefining the roles of project managers in the Project Management Office and converting
them to Product Owners. These newly minted Product
Owners started creating product backlogs and wrote user
stories for the teams they were designated to. For the first
time user stories, product backlogs, and acceptance test
concepts were being used across the enterprise.

Automated Testing Up Front

Another big change followed soon after—moving testing
up front in the process and automating it. At the time,
Getty Images had many black box UI testers who were
used to testing the product visually from the outside, and
did not have a high level of technical skill. This change
required the business to hire several new testers who could
program. Many internal people were also re-trained.

Single Week Sprints

With the fundamentals in place, the basic Scrum framework was rolled out across all of the teams. One of the key decisions here was to put all teams on the same sprint schedule. The leadership decided the best way to move the concepts along quickly was to make the sprints as small as possible. So they chose one-week sprints across the board. This was extremely uncomfortable for most people and teams. They wondered how they would write requirements, develop, and test in a week and actually get to **Done**—where **Done** meant a ready-for-production release story. This was precisely the Waterfall mindset that the short sprint cycles set out to break.

> ### DISCOMFORT AS A TOOL
>
> *Used well, like here, sprints can achieve very positive results, as it demands an entire re-imagining of how work gets done, as long as the integrity of the story—actual, workable software—is maintained. Here we see the unnatural one-week delivery cycle be so uncomfortable that it invited immediate focus and promoted future experimentation.*

It forced teams to move testing to the front, to automate, and to not get too bogged down by design up front. The transition was a lot of hard work. Teams had to figure out, in their own organic way, how to develop and test collaboratively, sometimes even at the same time.

Relative Estimation

All previous estimation techniques were set aside in favor of story points. Each team had their own scale, although most used the Fibonacci scale. Teams were coached on the value of relative sizing and use of actual figures was strongly discouraged. The idea that story points were a tool to help the team determine what they could get done in a week was the primary benefit that was taught.

Training

Getty Images realized that a wholesale Agile transition could not be achieved successfully without thorough training at all levels of the organization. To start with, all Getty Images IT executives, managers, and project managers were given an overview of Lean-Agile over the course of two days. After that, each team was required to find a ScrumMaster. The chosen ScrumMasters all received Certified ScrumMaster (CSM) training. Each team was also assigned a Product Owner from the Program Management Office, and each Product Owner received Certified Product Owner training.

Tools

Creating 25 product backlogs and allowing visibility across the enterprise of each backlog called for the adoption of a Scrum tool that could work across the enterprise. With so many backlogs, the teams needed more clarity and a single place to store the backlogs and product roadmaps. All development teams migrated to a new Agile enterprise tracking tool at once. The teams now had a new process and tools to help make their new approach visible in the organization.

EMBEDDING THE PROCESS AND PRINCIPLES

The Getty Images leadership recognized early on that once-off class training would not be sufficient to fully embed Lean-Agile principles and processes across so many teams and people, especially once those people left the cozy classroom, and went back to their work areas to face the reality of delivering product to market. To augment the initial training, Getty Images established an ongoing internal training program that incorporated a Lean-Agile steering committee, designated internal Agile coaches, and set forth a series of standing weekly training meetings.

> **LEARN INTENTIONALLY**
>
> *Informal but sanctioned learning drives intentional organizational change and frees us from overly focusing on the team level.*

The Lean-Agile steering committee was comprised of a cross-section of people from upper management and run by Jeff. The committee served as a check-in point to give visibility to progress made and to flag areas in the organization where internal struggles were occurring. Discussing these struggles was essential so that people could explicitly examine both the personal and team issues that were bound to occur with such a big organizational change.

Jeff and one other colleague were designated the go-to Agile coaches for the company. As coaches, they set up training sessions with each team to walk through Lean and Agile principles. The foundation of their approach was to focus on principles rather than the process—the "why" behind the changes. The coaches established weekly training sessions with all the ScrumMasters where they walked them through agile training content and scenarios. Jeff also instituted a weekly Lean-Agile Q&A which was open to everybody in IT. This was a standing meeting where people could come, ask questions, and bring their issues regarding the change to the table for discussion.

FROM SCRUM TO KANBAN

Getty Images worked in this Scrum mode for two more years with a continuing focus on coaching and mentoring the principles behind Lean and Agile development, continuous improvement amongst the teams, maturation in story writing, acceptance test driven development, automation, paired programming and team metrics (e.g. velocity, delivery of value). Along the way, there were two specific process issues that were never fully resolved.

For one, changing business priorities regularly made it difficult for Product Owners to have great stories ready at the start of a sprint. Although sprints were only one week, and that might seem to be a short enough iteration, it wasn't. Business needs would change within a few days.

The other issue was being felt in the development teams. Teams found themselves arbitrarily splitting work that was naturally larger than one week into multiple stories. Often, one or both of the smaller stories did not actually deliver business value in isolation. They were writing the stories to fit the sprint, rather than writing the stories to achieve business value. Teams were also reluctant to take on new work towards the end of a sprint (e.g. Thursday or Friday) because doing so meant that they would risk not meeting their sprint goal—a success measure that was actively monitored in the organization.

These two challenges were hampering the smooth flow of work and the delivery of business value.

EVOLUTION

Initially, Getty could not produce. Much of this was due to a lack of focus. Scrum helped teams improve and release, but as their organization matured, time boxes started to show their limitations: breaking down work beyond what is valuable/shippable and interfering with the natural flow of work.

TEAM KANBAN

As with the early adoption of Scrum, a few mature teams started working with Kanban. They put up physical kanban boards and started using Kanban in the context of their Scrum process. Kanban proved to be a highly successful model for these teams. They no longer needed to think about how to split a story arbitrarily, but could focus on story completion, swarming around a single story if required, and achieving consistent throughput and flow of work.

Seeing the success achieved by these teams, Getty Images management recognized that Kanban could help them address the anti-patterns that had evolved in the development teams. More and more teams switched to Kanban and dropped the Scrum framework altogether so they, too, could benefit from the more flexible approach to scheduling and having stories to implement that were actually meaningful. They did, however, retain many of the positive continuous improvement and communication practices such as retrospectives and daily standups.

Enterprise Kanban/Pull

While team Kanban started solving issues at team level, it didn't address the other big item. There was the remaining issue of changing business priorities mid-sprint, just before sprints started or faster than Product Owners could do any analysis. So in February 2011, Getty Images made another big leap. They switched to an enterprise pull model. Part of this transition included moving away from user stories, to what Getty Images called Minimum Valuable Features (MVFs), based on the concept of Minimum Marketable Features (MMFs), yet acknowledging that some features add value before being shipped to market.

There was one prioritized enterprise backlog of MVFs that was prioritized by the PMO and the pull was regulated by Development directors being responsible to pull from the top when a team had the capacity (and capability) to take on work. The pulling of work signaled a commitment to the work and Product Owners now only started to write stories once they were committed to.

No more sprints, no more arbitrary timeboxes—just continuous enterprise flow of features!

WHAT'S GOING ON WITH GETTY IMAGES NOW

After two years of using this enterprise pull model things are still going well. The concept of time-boxed sprints has completely disappeared. The focus is on flow. Their next step is to create better visibility into the metrics around time to market. The need to make cycle time visible has become key. More emphasis is now being placed on Cumulative Flow Diagrams to understand real value delivered across the business, and less on individual team velocity.

CONCLUSION

Getty Images Application Development looks, performs, and feels like a completely different company than it was in 2005. Morale runs high with employees as work-life balance improved and the stress of business pressure was greatly reduced, all the while delivering much more business value and throughput at any given time. In 2005 a world without project schedules, huge coupled releases, bug databases, highly collaborative one-hat teams, and shipping new software to the business on demand did not seem conceivable. But that is exactly the world of Getty Images today thanks to the foundation of Agile and Lean principles, and Scrum and Kanban as process frameworks for guiding that transformation.

SECTION 2
GRAPPLING WITH SPECIFICS

The stories In Part Two illustrate how to achieve specific things as you transition from iterative (Agile/Scrum) approaches to a flow-based (Lean/Kanban) workflow. If you have attempted this transition with your team, you may have encountered some challenges along the way. These stories will help you to develop a deeper understanding of some of these challenges, while sharing solutions other teams have used under similar conditions.

In *Managing Dependent Workflows With Kanban*, the software development team at Innvo had hit a wall in their search for continuous improvement with Kanban. This was brought on by cross-team dependencies. They tackled the problem by establishing fluid cross-team communication and workflow, even though the other teams did not necessarily use a kanban-based approach. As an added bonus, this change inadvertently enabled them to train cross-functional teams.

Taming the Recruitment Process with Kanban tells the story of the Human Resources (HR) team at Rally Software. They adopted kanban to help them understand their own operational process and to express, and address, their capacity limits. The understanding brought on by visualizing and limiting work enabled them to find a workable solution to improve the way they work and communicate with internal clients in the company.

Fundamo started as a mobile payments startup, initially well-funded by venture capital, that ran out of cash while trying to build their first release. *Scaling Scrum Down... and Up!* shows how, when they came dangerously close to shutting down, they took a good look in the mirror, trimmed out the waste, downsized their workforce, and came out with a product and a positive revenue stream within six months. Their continued success led to their acquisition by VISA in 2011.

The SocialText story combines the visual power of flow-based work principles and the transparency of social media. *Engineering Success through Social Swarming* traces the story of how their development team went from being paralyzed by dysfunctional work silos to being a single high-performing team that has built flexible and transparent communication and work planning into the very fabric of the system they develop.

MANAGING DEPENDENT WORKFLOWS WITH KANBAN

Evolution at Innovo Systems

Vital Statistics

Company: Innvo Systems Pte Ltd
Location: Singapore and Bangalore, India
Industry and Domain: Software development - applications for mobile handset manufacturers
Insights by: Siddharta Govindaraj it the founder of Silver Stripe Software Pvt Ltd, a company that develops products for teams Agile and Kanban teams. Based in Chennai, India, he has six years of experience with Agile, of which the last three years have been spent applying Kanban. He was a speaker at the Lean Software & Systems Conference in 2010 and 2011. He was nominated for the Lean Software & Systems Consortium's Brickell Key award in 2011. At the time of this writing, he was working with Innvo Systems.

Background

Innvo developed internet applications for mobile handset manufacturers. The company developed three products: a web browser, a messaging client, and software to enable the phone to communicate through the Internet. Innvo's key customers included handset manufacturers that wanted to bundle these applications with their phones.

This story covers the Innvo's experiences between October 2004 and 2006.

During these two years, Innvo maintained two divisions—a product department and a porting department, both based in Bangalore, India. The product department managed the roadmap for the three core products. Small, co-located agile teams of five to ten members developed each product. Each team was led by one or two senior developers who were experts in the product domain. The remaining developers were fresh out of college.

The porting department ensured products were available for the customer's handset model. Porting teams typically had two or three team members who were experts in mobile operating systems. There were usually two or three porting teams at a given time depending on the number of customers.

Additionally, a certification team of three people verified the products against industry standards of compliance. The certification team was equivalent to an external testing team. After a release, they would run certification tests on the release against an industry standard specification. This manual testing took about 2-3 weeks to run through the testing. The single small certification team received downstream work from all three product department teams. Because of the disproportionate size of the certification team this often posed a threat to the workflow causing a bottleneck at the certification process.

All the teams reported to managers in the company's headquarters in Singapore. The product teams all reported to a Product Manager, also based in Singapore, whose primary responsibility it was to maintain the long-term roadmap of the products. The porting teams reported to a Business Analyst who liaised with the customers.

At the time, Siddharta managed the Agile process in the web browser product team, fulfilling a variety of roles from coach to technical lead. During this period, kanban was still in its early days some of the principles were being discussed on forums, mailing lists and blogs, but "Kanban" had not yet become a formally described software development method.

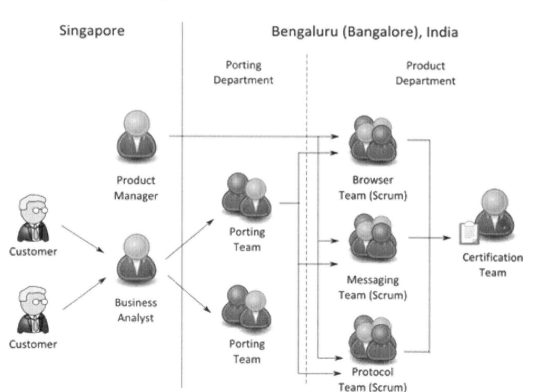

TALES OF CONTINUOUS IMPROVEMENT

BEYOND AGILE

Challenges

Managing dependencies between teams was one of the major challenges at Innvo. The image on the preceding page depicts these dependencies.

Customers collaborated with the Business Analyst to determine which products and features they needed on their handset. Once agreed upon, the subsequent require-ments were passed on to the relevant porting team in the offshore location to port the products. The porting team then took a build from the product team and ported it onto the customer's handset.

Sometimes the porting team required new features that were not present in the product, or they needed changes in the product to work around quirks in the handset architecture. In these cases, the porting team would add a feature request to the backlog of the product team.

There were also dependencies between the product teams themselves. The messaging client, for instance, used a rendering component developed by the browser team to display HTML emails. If the porting team asked the messaging team for a feature, and it required changes in this component, then the messaging team would need to add a request to the browser team's backlog.

These dependencies created some challenges for the product teams as they were often working on different things for different teams.

Visualizing the State of Work Items Within the Browser Team

The browser team created a board to visualize its completed work. Unlike a typical kanban board that depicts stages in the workflow, the board had columns for each team member. The board had three parts:

1. **Not Started Work** This is the planned work backlog.

2. **In Progress** A column for each team member shows what they are working on.

3. **Awaiting Verification** Once work was complete, tickets would be moved to the 'Customer' column for user acceptance (*a role Siddharta performed for the team*) before making a release to the certification team.

   Done Completed work was moved off the board to eliminate visual clutter and archived in a physical folder.

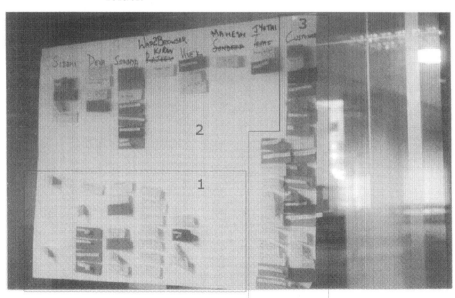

As different team members worked on an item they moved the stickies from column to column. For example, if one team member had finished some code and it was to be code reviewed or tested by another team member, then the sticky would get moved to the other team member's column. The visualization showed the workload of each team member at a glance.

The browser team worked on many different types of work:

⇨   New features based on the product roadmap

⇨   Requests from porting teams

⇨   Requests from other product teams

⇨   Bugs found after release

⇨   Bugs from certification failures

Exceeding Work-in-Progress

The picture on the previous page was from early 2005. A huge benefit of visualization is that many patterns emerge that one might not have noticed otherwise.

One thing that immediately jumps out is the

> **TEAM FOCUS**
>
> *Limiting WIP leads to less multi-tasking, which can help reduce context-switching, worker overload, and distractions. Eliminating these from our work and our teams' work allows focus, laying the groundwork for understanding and higher quality product.*

amount of simultaneous in-progress cards for some of the team members. The more senior team members on the left side of the board usually took on more work because they understood the system better. Before putting up the board, we didn't realize that such invisible overload was actually being counterproductive instead of helpful.

The picture to the left is from July 2005, a few months after the previous photograph. You can see that the team reduced its multi-tasking by more evenly distributing and balancing work across the team. The success of the board prompted the team to also put up a high level release board—the chart on the left—with the planned features for the next six releases.

Handling Emergency Requests from Porting Teams

Requests from the porting teams were almost always emergencies. Initially, the browser teams chose to apply a strict Agile process and did not allow new feature requests

BEYOND AGILE

within an iteration. However, this proved to be untenable since the porting projects were typically only around for 3 months each, thefore the porting teams could not wait an entire iteration (three weeks) for each feature request.

The teams eventually decided to allow feature requests from the porting teams mid-iteration and release the software as soon as these feature requests were ready. To do this, the web browser team ensured that they always had some capacity to pick up emergency feature requests. They achieved this by adopting the kanban principle of limiting work-in-progress— a concept the more experienced developers had picked up in their reading. Each person in the team was limited to working on a few features at a time, pulling features from the backlog only if there were no outside requests that took priority.

> **RESPECT REALITY**
>
> *Notice that the team always took "outside requests" as a priority over the planned development work. In Scrum, these surprise priorities are a violation to the team's workflow. However, Innvo's real business need could not function with rules that did not respect Innvo's unique needs. The Innvo team could see this and altered their process to ingest work as it actually arrived. Here, continuous improvement required looking at real work as it arrived and building a process to suit.*

As a direct consequence, they also decided to do away with the concept of an iteration commitment. Due to emergency requests and external dependencies, the delivered release might be different from the upfront iteration plan. However, the teams still continued with iteration planning meetings at the start of the iteration to establish a rough idea of what they wanted to do in the next three weeks.

Reducing Lead Time

Certain components of the browser product required domain expertise. Since not everyone in the team was a domain expert, they followed a code review policy that required a senior team member to review any code changes in specific components. As a consequence of this policy, some pieces of work spent days waiting to be reviewed.

> **DON'T HIDE FROM WASTE**
>
> *Continuous Improvement requires honest assessments of bottlenecks. In this case, Innvo identified a competency-based bottleneck. The solution rested not in expanding staff or overloading experts, but rather through leveraging existing competencies.*

Initially, the team was blind to this problem. After setting up the board, however, they found that senior team members' columns quickly became full with review tasks. Mapping their process gave the team visibility into the problem for the first time.

To resolve this bottleneck the team enacted a new policy that required pair programming when making changes to these components. This eliminated the need for code reviews and the team subsequently reduced the queue time on these work items.

Eliminating Bottlenecks in Other Teams

In the context of a single team, the process moved smoothly. The board helped the team visualize the status of work and identify blockages created by external factors. The team regularly delivered new, working software every three weeks. And, for some time they were content with that.

However, looking outside the team revealed more problems—and even greater opportunities to improve and be more effective. The browser team often waited quite long for the certification team to report certification failures. On closer inspection, it turned out that the certification team was overloaded. They had to check new features against the Open Mobile Alliance (OMA) test specifications. They also had to perform regression testing on older features against these specifications, using a test suite for each product that covered the specifications. Running these test suites was a manual, labor-intensive process. Each test run took the team approximately two to three weeks per product.

> **LOCAL OPTIMIZATION CAN BE BLIND**
>
> *Innvo found the perils of "local optimization." The browser team optimized their processes, but downstream work was still designed to accept work at the lower rate.*

Ironically, the faster the browser team delivered new features, the more overloaded the certification team became, leading to the total time for a complete release including certification verification to increase, despite the responsiveness of the browser team.

Since the browser team already had a large suite of automated unit tests, they decided to explore the possibility of automating the certification tests. They found that they couldn't use the existing unit test framework because of the visual nature of many of the certification tests, e.g. whether colors were displayed correctly on a particular mobile operating system. The team had to decide whether they wanted to stop browser development for a while and write a custom framework that would enable them to automate such visual certification tests.

Understandably, it was hard to convince management that going faster was actually the cause of the problem. As a compromise, the team agreed with product management to set aside a part of their development time to write the framework. This slowdown gave the certification team some breathing space, and allowed the browser team to automate some of the certification tests to trap more certification failures earlier in development. This "early" feedback loop dramatically reduced the load on the certification team and pushed forward product progress and improvement!

Conclusion

Innvo's experience suggests that a standard Agile process works well on its own within isolated teams. Yet, when complex interactions between teams were involved, Siddharta found that they needed to make incremental modifications to their process to reflect and accommodate these complex interactions. They accomplished this by incorporating basic ideas from the emerging Kanban methodology.

Some of these ideas included:

⇨ Limit Work-in-Progress, even within an iteration. This allowed them to tweak the process to handle changes in requirements and priorities mid-iteration.

⇨ Visualizing work is a powerful way of seeing previously hidden patterns and constraints.

⇨ Reducing the amount of time features wait in queues increases the rate of delivery.

⇨ Keep the whole system in mind. Delivering faster in one team at Innvo made things worse for the overall system.

Looking Back 8 Years Later

Innvo was a startup with investment backing. Shortly after Siddharta left Innvo, the investors decided to shut down the Innvo concern entirely. In Siddharta's personal reflection:

"It has been eight years since this project. Back in 2004, Kanban was yet to be a formalized development method. Is there anything I would do differently if I were doing this today?

The only thing I would add to the process is to use classes of service for managing the different work items. We were about

25% of the way there. We did recognize that there were different kinds of work items, and we used different colored stickies on the Kanban board for each type. However, we used the categories for visualization only, and didn't go further in using class of service for managing the backlog or the development process.

Class of service can be a very useful concept for teams that are servicing multiple stakeholders with different kinds of work items and different lead time requirements.

On the whole though, I'm pretty happy with the way the process worked out. "

~Siddharta Govindaraj

TAMING THE RECRUITMENT PROCESS WITH KANBAN
Rally Software's HR Kaizen

VITAL STATISTICS

Company: HR Department, Rally Software Development
Location: Boulder, Colorado. United States of America.
Industry and Domain: Software Development, Human Resource Management
Insights by: Jenny Shedd, Laura Lindenmeyer, Laura Burke, Diana Calderoni and Jean Tabaka

Rally's HR and recruitment team officially formed in March 2010. Each member assumed a unique role within the collaborative environment. The Senior Recruiters, Jenny and Diana, each had more than 15 years of experience recruiting for small, emerging companies. They worked closely with the internal customers (hiring managers). Laura Lindenmeyer was primarily responsible for operational systems and sourcing candidates, in addition to the role of Scrum Master. Laura Burke coordinated the candidate interview experience as well as team facilitation and process reviews.

BACKGROUND

Rally[1] is a company with an eye on maintaining optimal effectiveness, especially in periods of growth. The company works on its internal processes as it helps large organizations scale their software development activities. During 2010, as the HR and recruitment team supported Rally's growth, the team dealt with an increasing number of requests for recruiting. This meant keeping the recruiting flywheel running while figuring out how to streamline tools and processes to enable more effective hiring. In addition, the HR team felt unable to keep up with the competing demands from their customers—Rally's internal departmental hiring managers. There was no sense of priority: everyone needed everything immediately. This left the HR team immensely frustrated.

After seeing other parts of the company adopt a continuous flow model of work, and achieving great success with it, Rally's HR department decided it could potentially benefit from this new mode of working as well.

> **OVERWORKED**
> **IS**
> **UNDER-ATTENTIVE**
>
> *When Work-in-Progress is beyond a team's capacity, neither the team nor its members can scale or adapt their process. This can result in customers feeling under-served or ignored. It's a no-win situation despite the appearance of being very busy and attempting to always be responsive.*

What was driving this attempt at a new process? Due to the volume of hiring requests, HR team members found themselves working at an unsustainable pace. This resulted in many of them not taking lunch or breaks; they felt completely overwhelmed by what felt like an enormous workload that was not getting any smaller. The HR team itself also continued to grow, from 2 to 4 people in a matter of months, requiring them to find an optimal way of working together. One thing was clear. They needed a better process. It needed to address their ability to manage their capacity versus the amount of work being asked of them.

LACK OF PROCESS INSIGHT AND METRICS

The Rally HR team intuitively recognized that they were overwhelmed by the inter-dependencies and complexities of their internal recruitment process. But their existing work processes did not enable them to pinpoint specific bottlenecks or to effectively keep track of different hiring priorities for different customers. They were too overwhelmed to step back and analyze where their workflows were running counter to their success.

The following list of characteristics inherent to the nature of recruitment at Rally constrained the HR team's ability to organize and prioritize work effectively:

1.   At any time, there could be a large number and variety of simultaneous requests for hiring. These all seemed to require an immediate and equal response. The team handled requests coming from across the organization with no control over who was requesting what and by when. Those hiring managers who visited the team most often and squeaked the loudest received the

most attention. Consequently, the HR team prioritized these requests higher. This created even more pressure. Delayed requests from other departments became points of contention with the HR team and with seemingly competing internal customers.

2.   Any one department could have as many simultaneous job openings as they wanted. The HR team had no policy to limit these incoming requests, not even at the individual department manager level. This often created bottlenecks. And it was usually the same people in each department who would be involved in the recruitment process for each opening. Without intending to, they were creating their hiring own bottlenecks.

3.   The recruiting team knew its workflow was a multi-phase process involving a number of different parties and activities. All of these had to be coordinated. Each job opening followed the same typical framework: Locate the candidate; validate the candidate paperwork; get the hiring manager to approve the résumé; complete an initial phone call with the candidate; set up multiple interviews for the candidate; get feedback from each of the interviewers; and, either proceed to the next step of actually hiring the candidate or alerting the candidate that Rally would not proceed with the hire.

The HR team employed an online tracking system that helped identify candidate flow through the recruitment process. However, they had no visibility into how well they were meeting the hiring deadlines for departments. They couldn't readily identify whether a specific recruiter member of the team may need help with the number of requests coming out of a specific department. There were only four team members, all trying to do their best. But they had no way of knowing whether they were actually achieving any success.

And there were more woes for the team. In many of the steps in the hiring process, the team found themselves in a lot of "hurry up and wait" situations. They had neither control over nor visibility into either the unexpected wait times or the amount of rework (e.g. rescheduling candidate interview dates multiple times with the departments.) The team was becoming increasingly frustrated.

The key question that quickly emerged was: What to do about the lack of clarity and visibility into ongoing work happening throughout the process?

NO CLARITY, NO PEACE

Without clear insight into their work, Rally's HR staff could not explain to stakeholders the true costs of taking on new work, delays in existing work, and the value in past work.

This led to common business reactions like:

Volume-Based Prioritization – The loudest voice wins.
Self-Centered Optimizations – Team members focused solely on their own overwhelming workload above all else.
Suboptimal Workflow – In this case, departments could have as many open hiring requests as they liked, despite the overall toll it was taking on HR to fulfill requests.

TAKING THE PLUNGE WITH KANBAN

After identifying this root question, the Rally HR team began seeking solutions from other departments. They wanted to see what others used to provide clarity and visibility of their workflow. The team saw parts of the engineering group start to use Kanban and chose to try it as well despite not being an engineering team.

Initially, they experimented with aspects of Scrum, such as holding a daily stand-up meeting to briefly

> **CLARITY HAS IMPACT**
>
> *Here we see that Laura and her team were able to quickly understand and act on customer demands. This makes HR actions faster and more decisive. Prior to the visual control, the information on the board (the team's work) largely rested in the team members' brains — all of which were overloaded.*
>
> *The clarity of the board gave the team understandable and communicable work.*

communicate to one another what each individual was working on. They also collectively defined some high-level projects to improve their internal recruiting process and the overall candidate experience. These goals turned into specific strategic tasks like improving the company's career site. But the team struggled to organize their work into sprints. Despite their attempt at a Scrum adoption, they could never seem to find the time to complete their projects. And the frustrations just didn't go away.

Eventually their colleague, Jean Tabaka, an Agile Coach engaged to guide software development organizations worldwide, helped train and mentor the team to adopt Kanban. Jean specifically helped them to map out their individual and shared work processes in detail. The result of this effort was the creation of two Value Stream Maps that allowed the team to get started more effectively with Kanban.

The one value stream map reflected the overall recruitment process end-to-end. The second value stream map reflected each step required to set up an initial telephone screening with a candidate.

Both value stream maps revealed an alarming lag time between certain steps.

As Laura Burke recounts:

"There was a lot of work that I was doing that would 'put the ball in the other person's court' and then we often wouldn't hear back from the candidate for a week or more. Sometimes, our emails would get caught in their junk mail filter. Other times, they used an email address that they never checked. Just by paying more attention to reducing this time, we sped up our process and lost fewer candidates as well. Also, we realized that we were waiting on hiring managers to respond to résumés that we had submitted to them. Creating a kanban board helped us determine that it would be beneficial to limit the number of openings per hiring manager."

THE RALLY HR KANBAN BOARD

Armed with their new knowledge, the team set up a comprehensive chart of the main recruitment process on the wall in their work area. In a significant deviation from the common practice of Kanban in software development, they decided to limit Work-in-Progress (WIP) in one area only:

A hiring manager in a department could have only 1 open hiring request at a time.

The rationale behind this deviation was twofold. First, the team had identified that the administrative overhead of managing and juggling multiple hiring requests simultaneously was a key limiting factor in their ability to complete a single hiring request. They felt that addressing this point upfront would bring immediate efficiency gains in the hiring process.

WIP IS RELATIVE

*The Rally HR team examined their value stream and asked themselves some hard questions. The first being **What is our Actual Work?** It's not uncommon for team members in this request-driven environment to have dozens of unresolved requests coming in to them regardless of how many requests have not yet been completed.*

Here, HR realized that they were a bottleneck. Upstream far too many requests for their time were being generated. They rightly dealt with this by limiting the allowable size of their input queue.

Second, the team decided it was unrealistic to limit WIP on the various phases of the recruitment process itself. The nature of recruitment inherently required working on multiple requests at the same time. Why? Because there were so many wait times. While one request was on hold (e.g. waiting for a response from a candidate) it was quite possible to continue with another. Additionally, due to the urgency of some hiring requests, the team certainly couldn't justify declining a high priority request based on a WIP limit.

Having the wall chart with all their work-in-progress across every phase of the recruitment process clearly visible made a significant difference to their daily operations. The team started using the chart every day for their standup planning meetings. They could now easily see where they were stuck; what needed special attention; where tasks had been completed; where individual team members could take on more work; and, where they needed to stop taking on work. They also chose to use color-coding of stickies to help track the individual job opening and its tasks to be completed as they moved across the board. A colored dot represented who currently owned the item.

BOARD DESCRIPTION

The team set up an initial Kanban board shown on the next page.

• **Column 1: "Posting and Req Creation"** Write up the job description and determine how that person would

BEYOND AGILE

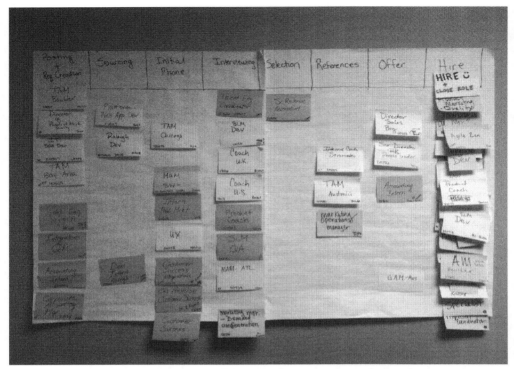

interact with the team. Identify the top 3-5 attributes that a candidate must possess to be successful. Post the job description on the Rally site, Craigslist, LinkedIn, job boards, etc.

• **Column 2: "Sourcing"** When a position requires a specific background, look for this person online, in the Rally HR database, in LinkedIn, etc.

• **Column 3 "Initial Phone"** The 1st phone screen with a team member, hiring manager and the recruiter.

• **Column 4 "Interviewing"** Bringing people in to meet with the hiring manager's team of interviewers.

- **Column 5 "Selection"** Completing final debriefs to decide on a candidate.

- **Column 6 "References"** Checking references on one or two candidates.

- **Column 7 "Offer"** Creating and sending out an offer.

- **Column 8 "Hire"** *Done!*

> ### STICK WITH WHAT WORKS
>
> *The Rally HR Team is unique. Their work and their context are not like other teams, even in their own company. For their work flow, the HR Team feels most comfortable with a physical board. A major goal of any process should be to optimize the team. Find the tool that works best for you in defining your process. Over time, you also learn how you continue to create clarity and visibility.*

Along the way, the team grew to love the visual representation of having a physical board with paper flip charts and sticky notes. The board visualized the current work state for our co-located team. And because everyone in the company at that time was also co-located, the board created visibility for each of the hiring managers who came to talk with the team. Starting with this physical board seemed like the right first step for the HR and recruiting team before working with an electronic board.

RETROSPECTIVE CADENCE

The team continued to use a timeboxed two-week cadence to check in on how they were doing. They also ran a "Squid" exercise from *Gamestorming*[2] to help them perform root cause analysis on their processes as a way to make sure they were not overlooking anything critical in the way they were conducting recruitment. This retrospective cadence felt right for the team though it was not built into their kanban board as an activity. This inspection cadence proved invaluable.

PRIORITIZING REQUESTS AND PROJECTS

> **THE ART OF KAIZEN**
>
> *The act of continuous improvement is based on small, understandable batches. This way, it helps to make work more predictable and over time allows for both process improvement and the refinement of the team's capabilities.*

With lag times between steps and the number of openings per manager now effectively reduced, the Rally HR team turned their attention to addressing another pain point in their process — the lack of clear prioritization across recruiting requests and general HR work and projects.

To help their internal customers understand the cost of the time constraints often placed on the HR team, the members of the team added Service Level Agreements (SLAs). These SLAs describe specific turnaround times for various aspects of the recruitment process. These

2   Dave Gray, Sunni Brown & James Macanufo, *Gamestorming: A Playbook for Innovators, Rulebreakers, and Changemakers,* (Sebastopol, O'Reilly, 2010)

SLAs are helping to create a clear and common understanding between the HR team and internal departments of the actual work involved in each new request.

In addition to dealing with ongoing recruiting requests, the HR team has a number of other activities to prioritize and manage. These include projects like sharpening up their recruiting site and advertising channels, training employees and hiring managers on the recruitment process, and providing guidance on interviewing candidates.

The team backlog for this work was never very organized. But now, in their annual planning sessions, they make a concerted effort to define backlog items for the year and quarter very clearly.

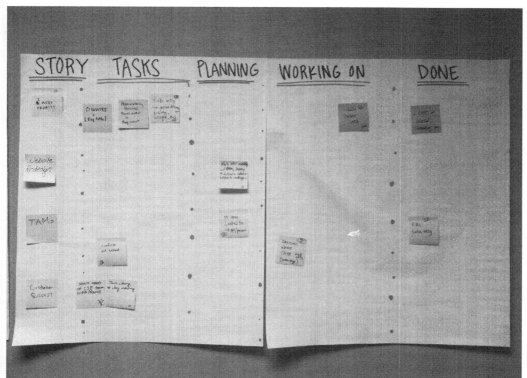

To keep the backlog clearly and rigorously ranked, the Rally HR team used paper on the wall with thin columns to physically constrain the backlog.

The areas highlighted in the next section were all defined in the improvement backlog as specific areas to prioritize and work on.

POTENTIAL AREAS FOR IMPROVEMENT

Swarming

The team has thought of using a "swarming" approach, i.e. having the group focus its energy on resolving a single problem or case to remove bottlenecks. For example, all team members could work on locating candidates for a specific role if the team member owning the particular job requirement is not having any success finding suitable candidates.

Swarming may also be particularly useful to address items on the board that have been stuck in a specific state for some period of time. Instituting an alarm to be triggered if something stays in a particular state too long could be the signal that the team is needed to swarm around the issue.

Metrics

Currently, the team measures the time it takes them to fill a position and the number of days they are past the requested date for the position. Measuring "Time to Fill" has enabled the team to plan their workload in advance better than before. And sure enough, "Time to Fill" has decreased since starting to use Kanban. This was true even when one member left the team. This is likely the result of reducing scheduling bottlenecks within hiring departments with the "Single Opening per Hiring Manager" rule.

However, the team wants to explore additional metrics to help them continue to improve their process.

Limiting Work-in-Progress

So far, the Rally HR team has not been limiting WIP in the traditional Kanban sense, apart from the "Single Opening per Hiring Manager" rule. This has been mainly due to changes in team size and an ever-increasing rate of incoming requests. However, the team fully appreciates the value of being able to limit incoming requests based on other objective criteria. As a result, they have experimented with a way to do just that within their context.

To set an initial WIP benchmark, they estimated the scope of the requisitions in progress based on complexity factors—*e.g. newly created position, hiring manager needs training, remote interviewing*—and assigned T-Shirt Sizes (XS, S, M, L, XL) to each request. Each size is assigned a number of points and added to calculate the current WIP. New items may not be pulled until the number of points drops below an acceptable level.

Although individual columns in the process are not yet being limited, this approach at least prevents the number of incoming requests from increasing in scope beyond their capacity.

Visibility and Prioritization

Although the Rally HR team greatly values the physical board in their work area, they are also experimenting with the electronic tool AgileZen a bit more, an evolution brought on by the expanding size of the company and its geographic spread. Using AgileZen would also benefit the HR team in another way. Other teams within Rally are already using AgileZen. Sharing their insights can help create a kanban board that provides even more visibility into the hiring process internally. It would also provide the executive management team and hiring managers a way to centrally prioritize openings.

WHERE ARE THEY NOW?

While still figuring out how to quantify their improvement, after 6 months of using Kanban, the Rally HR team felt like they had turned things around. And now, as the team continues to grow, the group as a whole continues to massage its processes. Everyone shares a sense of accomplishment and of positively contributing to Rally's success. In addition, as the team has made its process policies highly visible, the hiring managers feel part of the process. With a clear sense of where the HR bottlenecks are, the team can now watch the effects of constantly shifting priorities. This helps their internal customers recognize how those different needs impact the organization. And, with the process now mapped visibly, people from outside the team can collectively help prioritize the HR work. There is a sense of ownership and responsibility for all people involved in the hiring process, not just HR and recruiting.

SUMMARY

The Rally HR team members are excited about how this new way of working has helped them to create smooth flow of value to their internal customers. Based on their very positive experiences, they feel it could well become a gold standard for how HR/Recruiting is done in other organizations.

When asked if they have any specific advice for other HR departments keen to try Kanban, Laura Burke answers emphatically:

"Find something that you believe is worth limiting for the sake of effectiveness for the overall team. In other departments, it may make more sense to swarm around one thing and get it across the finish line.

In recruiting, you need to work on multiple openings simultaneously. For us, a WIP limit of 1 in any column would have been detrimental. Looking at our specific bottlenecks - the time it took to contact candidates and the time it took for us to get responses back from hiring managers—helped us determine what to limit. You'll have to do the same."

~ Laura Burke

SCALING SCRUM DOWN ... AND UP!

Fundamo's Adventures in Funding

VITAL STATISTICS

Company: Fundamo, a Visa Company
Location: Cape Town, South Africa, and Pune, India
Industry and Domain: Software development – mobile payments platform
Insights by: Karen Greaves

Karen Greaves started her career as a software tester working on Windows 2000. Since then she has worked as a developer, project manager, program manager, and head of a project office using variations of Waterfall. In 2002, she worked as the onsite customer for an eXtreme Programming team and was introduced to Agile. She is passionate about helping teams do Agile better, and has done so both within companies as a manager and internal coach, and now as an external coach with her own company Growing Agile. Karen is a Certified Scrum Trainer, and has been trained by David J. Anderson in Kanban. At the time of this story Karen was the Software Development Manager at Fundamo.

SUMMARY

Fundamo is a product development company in the mobile financial services market. Founded in 2000 in South Africa, they have been a leader in offering mobile payments to the largely unbanked population in developing markets in Africa. This story follows Fundamo's product development team as they deal with the pressures of having to scale down dramatically and then scale up again.

In July 2010, Fundamo was running low on cash and their future was uncertain. Investment funding on the new-generation mobile payments platform they had been building for two years had run out, forcing management to cut more than halve the development team. The version 1.0 release of the new product was late. Their first customer launch was delayed by months because of critical product issues.

By December 2010 things were looking up. The quality issues had been addressed and the first customers were able to launch with great success. And with license revenue finally coming in and more deals in the pipeline, management doubled the team size to keep pace with the anticipated growth.

And grow they did. In July 2011, Fundamo was acquired by Visa for $110 million, giving the business a further financial injection and raising expectations for delivery of new product functionality, faster.

But how are software development processes affected in such a changing funding landscape? How do you adapt to the changing expectations and capacity requirements without losing momentum?

In this story, Karen Greaves describes how Fundamo has relied on Agile and Lean software development techniques to find different ways for technical teams and their members to work together, not for the sake of changing process because they could, but because they simply had to adapt as the business context changed.

BACKGROUND

Fundamo is a company with a grand vision: bringing financial services to everyone by using mobile phones, especially to those living in parts of the world without a traditional banking infrastructure. The people who work at Fundamo love that they are part of changing people's lives, even though they seldom get to interact directly with the end-users of mobile payments in emerging markets like Africa and Asia.

Fundamo's direct clients are banks and mobile phone operators who want to implement financial services such as bill payments and airtime purchases using mobile technology. The Fundamo Enterprise Edition (EE) is an enabling platform that makes it possible for clients to rapidly implement mobile financial services using the core processing functionality provided by Fundamo and integrating with local financial services providers in the countries where the platform is deployed.

The Fundamo platform is developed and implemented by two separate divisions. The core product is developed by the Technology division, while integration with external systems and customized extensions are delivered by Professional Services. These two divisions follow different software development approaches and are located in separate buildings in Cape Town, South Africa.

Fundamo's Technology division has a fairly flat reporting structure. A small management team reports to the Chief Technology Officer (CTO) and all other staff report into that management team. Technology staff members are grouped in cross-functional Scrum teams of developers and testers working with Product Owners and Scrum Masters. These teams are co-located in one of the Fundamo offices in Cape Town. For a while, the Technology division also made use of remote team members in Pune, India.

The size and number of Scrum teams, as well as the number of Product Owners and Scrum Masters working with these teams, have had to change significantly over time in response to business growth. This story follows the course of these changes within the Technology division between 2010 and 2011.

ADAPTING WHEN THE FUNDING RUNS OUT

In July 2010, the Technology division at Fundamo found itself in trouble. Six teams with team members were distributed roughly evenly between Pune and Cape Town. They had been working for two years to create a new version of the Fundamo product that would be easy to configure, customize, and integrate with customer systems.

Venture capital was secured to cover the initial two years of development. The plan had been to rewrite the product using investment funding over the course of two years, thereafter using proceeds from product sales to drive further development. After two years, funding indeed ran out as planned, but the product was still not in production at the first client. As a result, teams were rapidly scaled down to a level the business could financially sustain which turned out to be 20 people, all based in Cape Town. They were tasked with putting out a release as soon as possible that would enable the first production client to at least go live.

> **SERVANTS OF MANY MASTERS**
>
> *Venture capital money gave Fundamo more people than necessary. Scrum gave them more rules than necessary. Those added together resulted in stagnation. When the overhead in people and rules was lessened, progress was possible.*

As often happens under such circumstances, there was also a significant change in management at this time. The Software Development Manager, single Scrum Master and Head of Architecture all left in July 2010. The Software Development Manager vacancy was filled immediately, but the others remained vacant for some time.

With far fewer people, many problems to deal with and a new Development Manager to boot, the teams worked many late nights and weekends trying to fix as many issues as possible before releasing the software. And although the release happened, it certainly was not the high quality release it could have been.

It was time to ask some hard questions about how things had come to this point.

The Technology division had adopted Scrum in 2008 when they started the rewrite. The teams had been using the practices of Scrum for incremental development and delivery, and the process up to that point had been structured around a large number of teams working in a distributed environment.

After the release, Karen Greaves, the new Software Development Manager at Fundamo, scheduled a division-wide release retrospective. This helped the remaining teams to talk about their frustrations with the release and how their development process needed to change to work with fewer people. They also had to acknowledge the painful fact that some core agile development principles had fallen by the wayside during the two years of fully-funded development. In some ways, complacency had set in, and key process and product development dysfunctions had not been addressed appropriately.

The fundamental insight from the retrospective was that the teams knew they had to return their focus to optimizing their development process. And as painful as it was losing half their teams, the new reality presented an opportunity to remove some existing complexities. This allowed for fairly significant process changes in a short period of time.

ESTABLISHING A PREDICTABLE RHYTHM

Before the staff reduction, the six teams worked on a single product backlog and shared two Product Owners and a single Scrum Master, both located in Cape Town. With all teams having members split between Cape Town and Pune, and Product Owners trying to manage multiple Scrum meetings for each team, keeping things organized was a tremendous challenge.

The solution to this had been to stagger the three-week sprints so that Product Owners could attend all meetings. This approach solved some problems, but created others:

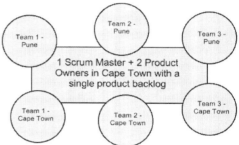

⇨ Nobody knew when a sprint started or ended without asking.

⇨ Sprint boundaries often became blurred and sprint planning meetings were often delayed so that teams could "finish one more story since the other team was still busy anyway."

⇨ Sprint retrospectives were rarely held.

⇨ Sprint reviews with stakeholders had been abandoned.

⇨ It was difficult to establish a predictable velocity for planning.

The staff reduction left Technology with only three teams, two Product Owners and one Scrum Master. It became easier to synchronize sprints again and they could now plan sprints jointly since all teams members were now collocated.

The problem with blurred sprint boundaries was addressed by fixing the sprint length to two weeks, with sprint planning

> ## SUNK COSTS
>
> *Fundamo had money and people, but they weren't communicating. The system they built was convoluted and ineffective. However, when they found themselves in trouble, they had already invested considerable resources into their existing processes. They could not throw out their investment, so they made the system even more convoluted.*
>
> *Psychologists and economists call this the Sunk Costs Fallacy – we keep investing money in a losing proposition in hopes that the additional effort will "fix" it.*

always on a Tuesday, and sprint reviews and retrospectives on a Monday. Having endured the problems listed above, the teams were excited by the opportunity to simplify. They themselves suggested the shorter sprints as they felt it would keep them more focused.

The impact of these changes was immediately evident. Sprints started and ended on time and velocity could be easily tracked. Retrospectives were held more regularly, and sprint reviews with business stakeholders were resurrected. An unexpected and welcome side-effect was that team members who had previously been complacent started championing the process again

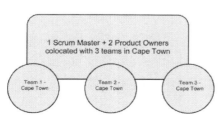

> **COHERENT SYSTEMS BREED COLLABORATION**
>
> *The issue was not the size of the organization, but the complexity they built into it. Six Team Fundamo was centrally controlled, had shifting arbitrary rules, and left no one in a position to effect change on a personal level. Three Team Fundamo gave the organization coherence because the coordination between teams was streamlined. It is the coherence of the system here that is giving developers freedom to act, managers the ability to grasp product needs, and the organization the ability to complete work.*

once they realized that radical changes could be implemented fairly painlessly and quickly.

MAKING TEAM DECISIONS

When there were six distributed teams, decisions about policies like the definition of done or when defects should be fixed, were either not made, or were dictated by management. Getting six distributed teams to reach consensus is hard.

After scaling down to only three collocated teams, this was much easier. Once the teams were all in the same location, joint retrospectives became possible. This enabled the teams themselves to identify issues that affected them all and to quickly agree on ways to address them.

Thanks to simpler and empowered decision-making, the teams now had an agreed definition of done and everybody committed to upholding it in their sprints. Everyone also agreed to stop delaying bug fixes to the end of the release and to fix them as soon as they were found. Both of these policies contributed significantly to improved

BEYOND AGILE

quality of work delivered by the Fundamo Technology teams.

REDUCING ADMINISTRATIVE OVERHEAD

Fundamo used ScrumWorks to manage the work of the six distributed teams. Both Cape Town and Pune maintained their own physical task boards to reflect their sprint work, but they were also synchronized via ScrumWorks. Once the teams were based in Cape Town only, the use of ScrumWorks initially continued as before.

The Customer Support team was using Jira to track customer issues. While considering the renewal of software licenses, management saw that it would be far more cost-effective to use the Greenhopper Agile project management plugin for Jira than to continue with a separate license for ScrumWorks. The teams were asked to try Greenhopper for a while. No complaints were received and the teams moved to Greenhopper.

> **FROM PAIN TO GAIN**
>
> *The teams hypothesized that having two tools was cumbersome and they experimented with a new tool. Since the teams were focused on improvement and not on making tools work, they came to the conclusion (even after spending money) that even the integrated tool was too cumbersome.*
>
> *The teams would not have done this in the previous environment that dictated process. In this case, they were able to make their own decisions based on real observed needs.*

A few weeks later, however, an exasperated developer complained about "that Hopper tool" during a retro-

TALES OF CONTINUOUS IMPROVEMENT

spective. He found adding tasks in Greenhopper much more cumbersome than in ScrumWorks and adamantly wanted to revert to the old tool. This led to the teams asking themselves the question: "*Why do we need to track tasks in a tool at all?*" Since they were now all collocated, the need to manage tasks electronically had actually long since been removed. They realized that they could make do with only physical task boards. Having agreed to that, the teams promptly proceeded to create their task board for the next sprint in half the usual time.

INTEGRATING ARCHITECTS IN THE TEAMS

Another benefit of having only three teams soon became apparent. At the time, Fundamo had only three software architects. These architects had previously been in a separate team, helping out when teams needed them. In practice, however, they were usually far removed from what was happening in the teams and therefore unable to help effectively when called upon.

With only three teams it was decided that the architects would join the teams. All architects now sat with their teams, attended all their sprint meetings and spent about half their time working with the team on the sprint. The rest of their time was dedicated to architectural initiatives.

The benefits were that architects were more in touch with what the work teams were doing, and therefore able to help out more easily since they had shared context. However, the model is still far from perfect, and some team members felt that if architects were not fully dedicated to the sprint they should not be considered part of the team. Sometimes it was difficult for architects to prioritize their work as they essentially belonged to two teams—their own Scrum team and a virtual architecture team. This sometimes led to them switching between concurrent tasks, a scenario clearly not ideal for individual work performance or satisfaction.

This is an area that requires further thought to find the best balance between architects collaborating effectively with the Scrum teams and feeling individually productive.

> ## WHO CAN JOIN
>
> *Here we see teams and the organization experimenting with opening up the team and allowing more voices. We see that the architects are clearly providing value, but questions about how we work, how we track our work, and what conversations we have remain.*

EXPANDING NEW APPROACHES TO MORE TEAMS

Six months after scaling down the teams, the core Fundamo product was in production at three client sites and revenue had started to come in. The changes had worked! Quality had improved due to teams being much more rigorous in their Scrum process and satisfied customers led to increased motivation all around. However, with an uptake from clients, there was an overwhelming demand for new features, and the teams were struggling to keep up. It was time to scale the teams up again.

After the previous experience of working with teams distributed between India and South Africa, management decided to keep the teams collocated and recruited in South Africa only this time. They also added more Product Owners and an additional Scrum Master, as these roles had been bottlenecks in the past.

Product and Technology now grew to four teams, each with its own Product Owner, and two Scrum Masters with two teams each. Having one Product Owner per team would allow individual Product Owners enough time to collaborate effectively with their teams while working closely with stakeholders in the Professional Services division. A separate Product Manager (one of the original two Product Owners) acted as Chief Product Owner and represented the product management team to senior management and external clients.

The fact that the Technology division was growing again, fuelled by funding generated from their earlier successes, was very positive. However, as with any change, this new context brought its own challenges.

> ### REAL-TIME EXPERIMENTATION
>
> *Fundamo is experimenting with a mission-critical feature: onboarding. Onboarding is different everywhere, so there are no real direct best practices to apply. Onboarding is cultural, contextual, and highly personalized.*
>
> *Fundamo's willingness to experiment to allow new hires to become comfortably acculturated is interesting because it is an extreme case of healthy process experimentation at all levels.*

CREATING A NEW TEAM

The first challenge was deciding how best to create the new team to maximize their product learning and consequently their productivity. Since Fundamo was expecting to hire one to two people per month over a period of time, new team members would not be able to start together.

The elected approach was to expand the existing three teams over a period of four months by adding newly hired people to those teams. Once the teams were big enough to split into four equal-sized teams, a fourth team was created out of a few members of each of the existing teams. Each team was left with a good mix of new and experienced people.

As to be expected, the new team struggled initially while they grew accustomed to working together. Management supported them by adjusting their delivery expectations and providing a safe environment in which they could fail and learn. From the outset, this new team learned to use failure as a learning experience, rather than something to be avoided.

Six months after being created, the team was well-integrated, and displayed an openness and a much more mature attitude to failure than some of the well-established teams.

Grooming 75% Waste

After growing to four teams, Fundamo continued to use a single backlog. The thinking was that joint backlog grooming would help all teams understand the backlog, enabling any team to work on any story.

It soon became apparent, however, that people were not focused during grooming. Grooming discussions happened mostly between a few individuals who had been at Fundamo for a long time. The large group format, combined with having a number of new people with little background knowledge, was not conducive to successful backlog grooming. The reality was that each team would only work on 25% of the stories they groomed. The other 75% of the time they spent grooming was waste. It was not at all surprising that people were disinterested.

> **WHAT? COHERENCE AGAIN?**
>
> *Thematic work segmentation allows people working on a release to not only understand the individual features being released, but to build a narrative around that release. In this case, working with a release theme not only gave the developers more context into what they were building, but also helped eliminate long, confusing meetings and other overhead.*

Along with team feedback that grooming wasn't working for them, one-on-one feedback from new senior developers revealed that they were struggling to understand the system. The core Fundamo product is extensive, and teams often worked on different product areas within the same sprint. This made it difficult for new developers to build deep knowledge of any one part of the system.

Although Fundamo wanted to retain the flexibility of having teams that could work on any part of the product, a compromise was needed that would help address the issues above. It was agreed that each team would have a singular focus area for the duration of a release (three to five months). The focus area would be a business theme and would enable the team to understand both the business domain and the code in that part of the system well. This would be a more achievable task for a new developer than learning the entire system piecemeal.

This change naturally meant that it was predetermined which features would be developed by which team and allowed for grooming to be held within the team. This approach was far more successful than the big team grooming form before, clearly evidenced by the increased levels of engagement during backlog grooming.

Empowering Product Owners

Previously, when Fundamo had six teams spread between Pune and Cape Town, they had only two Product Owners. This placed all responsibility for business analysis, interaction with teams, the organization and customers on the shoulders of only two people. The two Product Owners dealt with this as best as they could, the one taking on liaison with senior management and clients, the other dealing with all team collaboration and interaction.

Having learned the hard way that this setup was a sure recipe for bottlenecks and missed requirements, management introduced additional Product Owners at the first possible opportunity to do so, working towards the goal of enabling each Scrum team to have a dedicated Product Owner.

But how do four Product Owners and a Product Manager—one of the original two Product Owners—collaborate successfully on a single product? The Product Owner role is, by definition in Scrum, designed to be a single empowered decision-maker. This was a new challenge for Fundamo to wrestle with.

For the teams it was clearly beneficial to have a single Product Owner with whom they could build a strong working relationship and who was accountable for answering their questions. For the first time ever, Product Owners now actually had enough time to spend with their teams to clarify requirements.

HELPING DEFINE THE PRODUCT OWNER

The Product Owner role is often poorly defined and leads to the downfall of many Agile projects. A large factor in Product Owner missteps is a large, undifferentiated backlog and stakeholder management. The Product Owner ends up being responsible for the whims of the customer, the demands of the team, and the backlog itself.

In creating a Thematic Release System, Fundamo was able to give the Product Owners something to fall back on. Items that did not conform to the release theme could easily be scheduled for a later release.

BEYOND AGILE

But what to do when the solution is not clear? Since the group of Product Owners was collectively responsible for delivering the core Fundamo product, it was difficult for them (and the teams!) to know which of the five Product Owners was ultimately responsible for final functionality decisions and global product or release decisions. This was particularly true when they disagreed about either the requirements or appropriate release strategies. The Product Manager – unofficially acting as Chief Product Owner – was mostly out of the office liaising with customers and prospects, and therefore seldom available to make just-in-time decisions. There was no explicit delegation of authority to the other four Product Owners for matters that went beyond individual team stories. As a result, more than a few business value decisions were likely delayed beyond the "last responsible moment."

To great all-round relief, this was partly resolved when the teams started working on predetermined product themes. Each Product Owner could now manage their own backlog and had full responsibility for any functional decisions made in that area of the product.

However, this still left a gap in ownership for the release as a whole. The Product Manager was still primarily externally-focused and not involved enough with the details of feature implementation to make timely decisions regarding the release.

LESSONS LEARNED THE HARD WAY: CONCLUSIONS

Long-term funding, while attractive, can be damaging.

If you are not delivering to production early to generate revenue, the product remains untested, both in terms of real-world validation of product quality and the relevance of product features. This is typical of major software rewrites. Instead of embarking on such a closed, funded development, rather find ways to release early and incrementally improve the current product while continuing to ship to production. Losing feedback from actual customers is an agile failure pattern that can cost you dearly.

Optimize, rather than upsize, your teams.

Often growing teams is the first option you consider when you want more capacity. Before you do so, be aware that the added complexity of more teams may slow you down rather than speed things up. If you must grow, find ways to reduce complexity, like focusing teams on business themes over a medium term to enable them to absorb product knowledge effectively. Better yet, before assuming you need to grow, look critically at how you are using your capacity today. Better prioritization, along with teams with deeper knowledge, might mean that you don't need additional teams.

Shared accountability creates confusion and delay.

On large products with many teams, having a team of Product Owners may be one way to distribute the workload inherent in this role. However, their effective-

BEYOND AGILE

ness will be limited if they are not empowered to make autonomous decisions. Consider other patterns, such as a single Product Owner supported by a team of business analysts, user experience designers and systems analysts. Alternatively, establish individual accountability for each Product Owner by segmenting the product and/or business domain along clearly-defined boundaries. Whatever pattern you choose, it needs to be clear to all involved how product and release decisions will be made.

Empower people to inspect and adapt.

In many development organizations, Agile is the new status quo. Although teams may be experiencing significant pain because of process limits and dysfunctions, they are often not empowered to change things when needed. This happens particularly if Agile is implemented top down and specific practices are prescribed, rather than empowering teams to learn from their mistakes and make their own improvements.

Teams need to be taught how to identify root causes and take small corrective actions. For Agile to be sustainable in the long run, teams need to be taught the discipline and skills to improve continuously, rather than being taught a set of practices that may or may not apply as their context changes. Analysis: Teach a man how to fish (skills to improve), don't just give him the fish (the rules to apply).

ENGINEERING SUCCESS THROUGH SOCIAL SWARMING
WikiCulture at Socialtext

VITAL STATISTICS

Company: Socialtext

Location: Palo Alto, California, United States of America

Industry and Domain: Enterprise Social Software

Insights by: Eugene Lee and Shawn Devlin

Shawn Devlin

As Socialtext's Chief Architect, Shawn Devlin excels at capturing and communicating complex systems, not just to developers, but to those not programming. He has an architectural mind that enables him to create code and designs that are tight and rational. He's passionate about applying Scrum and agile methodologies to help software teams become more effective through continuous improvement and robust practices. He has acted as an agile coach and development lead that has supported senior sales executives and led technical teams in a number of software companies. Shawn holds a BMath degree from the University of Waterloo.

Eugene Lee

Eugene Lee was the Chief Executive Officer and a member of the Board of Directors at Socialtext. Lee oversaw day-to-day management and operational control over all aspects of Socialtext's business, including driving product direction and development, strategic alliances, and scaling the sales, marketing and support organizations globally.

Lee came to Socialtext from Adobe Systems, where he led Adobe's enterprise marketing and vertical market segments. Previously, he held several executive leadership roles at Cisco Systems, ranging from Vice President (VP) Worldwide Small/Medium Business Marketing to VP Worldwide Enterprise Marketing. Lee also held key management positions at Banyan Systems, including General Manager for the messaging business unit. He co-founded Beyond Inc., developers of the award-winning BeyondMail product, and holds four patents in messaging, workflow and privacy technologies. Lee has a B.A. in Physics and B.S. in Engineering and Computer Science from Harvard College and an MBA from the M.I.T. Sloan School of Management.

BACKGROUND

When Eugene Lee joined Socialtext in 2007 as CEO, he found a company with an exciting product that was helping companies to soar by tapping into the power of shared internal knowledge and expertise. But the same magic wasn't happening at Socialtext, particularly in the Product Development unit—the very unit responsible for developing the company's enterprise collaboration products.

For just over six months, Product Development had been operating without a Vice President of Engineering (VPE) after the departure of the previous incumbent. Eugene found himself having to stand in as VPE as much as his executive role allowed. In the absence of clear technology and people leadership, a fundamentally disabling workplace culture had come about that was preventing the unit from delivering on its product development goals successfully.

Tribalism could be found at the heart of this disabling culture. Product Development consisted of a number of siloed project teams consisting of developers, testers and documentation staff separated by function (development, testing, project management, etc.). These teams were (and still are) distributed across the world, all working from home offices and relying on tools like Skype, internet chat, and the Socialtext platform itself for communication.

These project teams had evolved into clusters of friends – tribes—each operating with its own tools, rules and practices, often lacking clear delivery metrics. New members had been hired into these teams through known referrals without a clear match between individuals and the greater company culture.

BEYOND AGILE

With this tribal thinking came the usual associated behavior: divisive relationships between different tribes, lack of transparent communication and the absence of a cohesive purpose. For a software company building its future on enterprise collaboration, this was an almost surreal position to find itself in. But perhaps a software company building its future on enterprise collaboration was also uniquely positioned to address this unhealthy dynamic?

They succeeded in doing just that: transforming the dysfunction into a smoothly-operating distributed team that is able to develop and deliver software on-demand with reliable predictability, high quality and a shared vision of their product and purpose.

THE TRIBE IS DEAD, LONG LIVE THE SWARM

It was clear to Eugene that the tribes (and the associated "us and them" thinking) would have to go if Socialtext were to successfully address the dysfunction in the Product Development unit. They needed to build a well-functioning team with focus that could build value for customers on a timely basis.

But where to start? As CEO cum temporary VPE, his first order of business was to insist on a culture of transparency around team output, and predictability where a team deserving praise based on their performance would get it publicly. If criticism was in order, that would also happen publicly. As cross-tribal relations were already a sensitive issue, transparency must be brought about in a very delicate manner. To overcome such delicate team relationships, Socialtext needed practices and processes that communicate information explicitly and openly.

Fortunately, some of these practices were already taking root in Product Development. Just before Eugene joined as CEO, Shawn and other senior developers had internally cultivated their own vision of a "swarm." Namely, a swarm is a team working in an intensively collaborative environment, with no silos, some levels of specialization where required and rotating pairs of developers and testers gaining exposure to diverse product areas through story assignments.

> **TOP DOWN TO BOTTOM UP**
>
> *A company has roles: executive, managerial, production, etc. Eugene's "insistence on transparency" was a top down edict to drive culture. However, it was met by an already existing bottom-up movement for collaboration. In this way, both Eugene and the developers were working toward a collaborative environment.*

Together, the switch to a whole team approach and Eugene's executive insistence on transparent development metrics started showing some positive results. Within four months of introducing these principles, a number of people in the various tribes who were actively resisting the changes and not pulling their weight, left the company of their own accord.

With the cultural dissonance resolved in a peaceful manner and a newfound collaborative and united team environment in place, Socialtext was ready to embark on a major undertaking. At the beginning of 2008, they began to develop their Enterprise Social 2.0 product, a nine-month project with major expansions to the existing product. The timeline and scope is a demanding expectation, and the team would have to work hard and quickly in order to meet this deadline. The fragility of the tribalistic team would have never been able to uphold this level of stress, but this project would be the first real test to the newly established team structure and culture – the swarm.

BALANCING DEMAND AND SUPPLY IN ITERATIONS

The project was a great success for the Socialtext Product Development team. By September 2008, as required and needed by the business, they managed to deliver a high quality product. Delivering real customer value as a cohesive team for the first time certainly was a major step forward for them. This was a huge win for the team.

Since the swarm is a newly developed way for people at Socialtext to work and relate to each other, the new process naturally had some kinks to work through. The development team had done very well to deliver on their overall commitment, proving to the product managers that they could reliably deliver features as scheduled per iteration. However, as product managers began to see features being delivered sooner than before, it appeared to whet their appetite for rapid feature development, resulting in a growing conflict between product managers and developers, specifically around the introduction of stories mid-sprint and the length of iterations.

At the start of the project they had chosen to follow a typical agile Scrum methodology with a two-week sprint cycle:

Monday	Kick-off Mondays!	P.O. + team plan iteration and developer/tester pairs pull the work they want
Tuesday		
Wednesday	Code Complete!	
Thursday		Bug fixing
Friday	Delivery!	Bug fixing

FINDING TIME TO PREPARE NEW STORIES MID-SPRINT

Typically, by the second Thursday of the sprint, the Product Owners would be busy reviewing the current sprint stories and planning stories for the next sprint. At this point they would usually need input from developers for on-the-fly story grooming and estimation.

But the developers were seldom available because they were usually fixing bugs that were preventing a current sprint story from being completed. The remote distributed nature of the team added to this challenge, as developer availability was more difficult to manage. Having all developers available in one room to discuss stories with the Product Owner would certainly have helped!

This resulted in Product Owners substituting their own broad estimates – estimates that would often be revised dramatically by developers after the following Monday's planning meeting. This in turn forced Product Owners to make spot decisions about stories to drop from the sprint, or left the team with no choice but to take on stories that were actually too big for a single sprint.

SWAPPING STORIES MID-SPRINT

Up to this point, the development team had been using a moving average of points done for three iterations to calculate the velocity per iteration. This metric had proven to be quite accurate, but depended on Product Owners upholding the original iteration commitment by not adding to or removing stories from the sprint once it had started.

Unfortunately, often as a side-effect of story estimates being changed dramatically after Monday sprint planning, it became common for Product Owners to drop planned stories and add new ones to sprints, sometimes as much as a few days after the start of the sprint. Some Product Owners also added stories mid-sprint simply because they were keen to have them developed as soon as possible, having become increasingly enthusiastic about using

> ### TEMPORAL TENSION
>
> *The tension between iterative systems and the natural flow of work was being experienced by Socialtext. The iteration helps normalize communication and, in some cases, give teams focus. But the organization's work flow doesn't always work cleanly with team sequestration during a sprint.*

Agile for rapid feature development, thereby breaking a core principle of Scrum—maintaining the integrity of the sprint commitment.

As can be expected, all this made it increasingly difficult for the developers to maintain an accurate and predictable velocity that Product Owners could, in turn, rely on for release planning.

All around, sprints seemed not to be working for the Socialtext team all that well anymore.

EVOLVING FROM SCRUM TO KANBAN

Typically in Scrum, challenges such as these are addressed by experimenting with sprint length. Surely, with more time during a sprint, developers would be more readily available for estimation and heavily modified story estimates—*Kick-off Mondays would be a thing of the past?*

The swarm experimented with three-week and four-week sprint cycles. The developers quickly found that four weeks were too long for them, and seemed to drag with some loss of focus, and settled on three weeks. This certainly led to some improvement, as there were more days available for actual development between the Kick-off and Review meetings, and developers were more readily available for story preparation.

However, the product managers weren't keen on three-week iterations, as it meant they had to wait longer to introduce new features into the story pipeline.

Some of the team members had heard about Kanban at various conferences and suggested they try the concepts of limiting Work-In-Progress and making work visible instead of using sprint cut-offs to control the flow of work through the team. The major benefits of this would be that developers would be available on an ongoing basis to assist Product Owners with estimates, and Product Owners would have complete control over scheduling and prioritization of features for continuous delivery.

Fully supported by the new VP of Engineering, Shampa Banerjee, who had since joined the business (January 2011), the development team started experimenting

KAIZEN CULTURE

Kaizen Culture is a culture of continuous improvement. Socialtext showed a relentless dedication to improving both product and process

with iteration-free, on-demand releases instead of following their usual defined Scrum cycle. Seeing that this was an experimental phase, they also implemented continuous integration of newly developed features and started using their internal wiki to publish and maintain user acceptance tests.

Within six to eight weeks, work was flowing through the team at a regular pace that satisfied both the developers and Product Owners.

▷ **With Kanban the team felt as productive as before but without all the drama.**
   ~ Eugene Lee

ADDING THE SOCIAL SAUCE

Having seen great promise in this new way of working, the Socialtext team started looking around them for tools to help support this new, visually transparent way of working and found them in their own backyard. Instead of using any of the Agile or Kanban tools that have sprung up in recent years, they decided to use their own platform instead to create a shared, highly visible platform for work in progress.

This platform has evolved into an ecosystem of workspaces, automated processes and integrated tools that ensures that everybody in the organization (yes, *everybody*, even those pesky Marketing and Sales people!) knows what's happening in Product Development and is able to act on that knowledge appropriately and timely.

SEEING WORK IN PROGRESS

A workspace is a collection of pages that are grouped together within the Socialtext collaboration platform. At Socialtext, all information related to product development is maintained and tracked in workspaces to create dynamic, up-to-date views to show status and progress of all stories in the development pipeline.

It all starts with the Product Management workspace where product managers and Product Owners focus on feature design. Once a story has been fleshed out, the Product Owners publish a page for each potential story to be developed in the Development workspace. Each page is tagged with keywords to group related stories together under themes. Each page also has a potential release tag. Release tags are (fun!) alphabetical iteration names like *Jonas Brothers* or *iCanHaz..*

Story pages are based on a template (itself evolving as needed) that provides for typical elements like prerequisites, user acceptance tests, examples and rough size estimates expressed in T-Shirt sizes by senior developers who work with the Product Owners.

> ## QUALITY FROM WITHIN
>
> *Socialtext's teams had more fun as the clarity around their work increased, since software development is knowledge work, and since knowledge work comes from our brains, and since our brains work better when we are not stressed or agitated – there is a direct relationship between enjoyment of work and quality product.*

Each development task associated with a potential story also has its own page. A task page includes details about the technical implementation, the status of the task and a more refined size estimate expressed in points. Task pages are automatically tagged with the same theme and release keywords used to tag the stories.

Finally, WAFLs—standard customizable plugins for the Socialtext collaboration platform—are used to aggregate and display progress information in different views suited to different roles (Product Management, Development, Testing). For example, using the tags applied to pages and the appropriate WAFL, a new Socialtext page is created automatically for each planned development iteration. The page combines the stories, tasks, estimates and status information in table format, and keeps all the information up to date as each source page is updated by a product manager or developer.

These iteration pages are visible to anybody in the company interested in seeing what they're working on and how well the work is progressing. But they're not restricted to the WAFLs table view. There are also various Kanban-based views available that enable people to view the same information in the way that works best for them.

A popular view is CorkBan. It provides a horizontal workflow view that can be embedded in other pages, enabling people to see development status from their own dashboards, if they so choose. Eugene himself uses CorkBan as part of his personal Socialtext dashboard.

Inspired by the visibility it gives them, some non-development employees have also started using CorkBan to manage their own work with Personal Kanban.

TALKING ABOUT WORK IN PROGRESS

A key part of successful collaboration at work is empowering people to actively participate in conversations about work, not merely passively viewing information that is shared with them.

This is where Socialtext Connect comes in. The Connect plugin provides an additional social layer that users of the Socialtext platform can use to create activity streams and automated bots that respond to specified triggers in the activity streams.

BEYOND AGILE

The Socialtext team has used their Connect plugin to great effect to facilitate conversations about work in a variety of ways, from making daily standup meetings more productive to enabling non-technical users to provide feedback directly to the technical team.

DAILY STANDUPS

The daily standup conversation is key to Scrum and other agile software development approaches. It is intended to be a short update on work in progress where people can raise obstacles that are preventing them from getting work done. In many teams, however, this meeting often becomes a drawn-out affair that doesn't add all that much value. The Socialtext daily standup fell into this trap.

With all team members working remotely, often in different time zones, they had already found a novel and flexible way of conducting their standup virtually, using what they call the LogBot—a bot the team had created with Socialtext Connect. Team members use voice chat to share their status and progress with each other and the LogBot would automatically record the conversation in the team standup page on the Socialtext wiki for later reference.

However, the meeting was turning into a long series of progress and status updates, rather than an effective conversation about stumbling blocks and solutions. To streamline things, team members decided to rather add the standard progress and status information to the wiki before the standup meeting, leaving the virtual chat time for conversations about challenges and areas where people needed help. By changing the way they approached their standup, they increased the quality of the conversation significantly—*and shortened the meetings from 30 to about 10 minutes!*

FEEDBACK FROM INTERNAL USERS

With internal users actively using the Socialtext platform, it creates an ideal opportunity for the Product Development team to elicit feedback from them about the software.

To make it easy and fun for users to provide feedback, the Product Development team used Socialtext Connect to create dedicated bots to take the tedium out of logging bugs. The BugBot automatically creates bugs in the bug tracking software from a text update accompanied by the *#bug* tag. And if you don't want to spend time typing, you can use Sally Socialtext to do it for you. All you type is the *#sally* tag and Sally will let you fill in the bug details just by speaking!

> **KNOW YOUR CULTURE**
>
> *Socialtext lives wiki culture. Their solutions therefore are borne of the wiki. What solutions naturally attach to your culture?*

With everybody in the organization being able to view the Product Development activity streams, it makes for a very open and transparent environment for feedback. Feedback doesn't just disappear into a black hole without a response. Others see bugs being logged in the activity stream, thereby creating a visible shared expectation for a resolution.

THE EFFECT OF DRINKING THEIR OWN CHAMPAGNE

As Eugene recounts, using their own social platform to this extent has created an "ambient awareness" in the organization of the challenges faced by the technical teams. Client-facing teams who would previously have had no insight and little empathy with the difficulties in software engineering, have developed a deeper appreciation for the work they do.

More significantly, teams like Marketing and Sales who rely on the delivery of new features to grow the Socialtext business now have a clear view of plans for upcoming releases, with full access to business requirements, examples and user information to produce client collateral. This has greatly helped them to plan more effective launches and campaigns.

> **VIRAL UNDERSTANDING**
>
> *Having similar, but individually optimized, visual controls throughout Socialtext helps all segments of the business communicate. Better understanding of work by any individual (developer, sales, management) leads to more targeted and timely product development.*

But it's not just Product Development sharing information with the rest of the business—*although they certainly started a trend!* Some of the business teams have also started sharing information about their work and events, like Services and Business parties, and feedback received from customers. This in turn feeds real customer input into development.

Just by sharing information visibly and transparently among themselves, in fact, they have seen and solved work problems that previously went unnoticed. Sometimes improvements are the result of sudden discoveries, like somebody outside of Product Development noticing that a particular story is missing an important requirement for a particular market segment. At other times, improvements have come about slowly and incrementally as people use and adjust the social ecosystem to work smarter.

Finally, the clearly visible roadmap that is reviewed by the Leadership monthly has made it unequivocally clear to everybody in the business what the key priorities are for the company. And everybody can see these goals being achieved. This certainly was the case in 2011 when the whole company watched the development and first on-site application of an ambitious data migration tool go off without a hitch. What a moment to celebrate together!

LEARNING TO LET GO OF RELEASE DEADLINES

As CEO, Eugene was initially not entirely comfortable with one of the side-effects of a more flexible approach to delivery—the inability to predict exact release dates. Although he was thrilled by the efficiency benefits of the evolution from Scrum to a continuous flow of work and fully trusts in the team's ability to deliver, he did ask them to compromise from time to time by doing "release pushes."

A release push was typically three to four weeks long, with a period of regression testing before the release date, despite the fact that continuous integration of features eliminates the need for regression testing. He acknowledges that these release pushes primarily fulfilled a personal need to counteract the angst he intermittently felt at the absence of targeted deadlines and tangible delivery and productivity metrics.

Since the team has shifted to on-demand feature delivery, these fears have however been allayed. The built-in metrics in Kanban provide in-depth, explicit efficiency feedback. And being able to deliver small changes rapidly to customers has been a great help to the sales, support and product management teams. At Socialtext, the development team no longer needs to adhere to minutely-planned, strictly controlled release cycles to satisfy customers. Customers are satisfied because they can get what they need, when they need it.

SECTION 3
GOING DEEPER

Our final three stories delve deeper into the psychology and practices of teams that have reached a hard-earned level of maturity in their application of the principles of flow-based continuous improvement. These teams are not paragons of virtue to emulate, however. All of them have made mistakes at some point or another. All of them have tried changes that did not work as well as they expected. But all of them show us what a deep commitment to continuous improvement can look like.

In *A Journey to Collaborative Ownership* we tell the story of Brainstore, a now defunct business that productized its expertise to help customers solve complex problems. They grew too fast when times were good and weren't able to scale back sustainably when times were bad. They used Lean and Agile to help restructure the company in response to internal and market changes, but made a critical mistake in the way they went about it. They got back on their feet again and tried again, however, armed with precious knowledge attained from past failure.

CCRTV is a Catalan media software company with internal clients. They first implemented Scrum to establish a structured way of handling client needs and formalizing them into prioritized projects and deliveries. They continued, however, to struggle with aligning development teams to individual projects and coordinating and prioritizing requests from multiple Product Owners. In *Taming Uncertainty in the Media Industry*, we see how CCRTV used metrics, visualization, and flow to turn chaos to clarity.

Shifting to Collective Ownership of Quality is the story of FiftyOne, an e-commerce company based in Tel-Aviv. It is a success story about turning a work atmosphere previously focused on avoiding disappointment into one of self-driven productivity and trust across the organization. This positive trust-based environment made it possible for Product Owners to relax their need for definitive commitments, enabling the organization to adopt a classical pull system, with people individually motivated to create value.

As you will see, the definition of success in each case depends widely on circumstances, leadership and often, the organization's ability to adapt culturally. There is no perfect end state. Just when you think things are running smoothly, new challenges spring up, the business context changes or people leave and team dynamics change.

The key is how you respond to these changes. We believe the principles with which we started this book offer some very real and sustainable ways to respond effectively to change.

A JOURNEY TOWARD COLLABORATIVE OWNERSHIP
Changing Context and Changing Culture at Brainstore

VITAL STATISTICS

Company: BrainStore
Location: Biel, Switzerland
Industry and Domain: Innovation and Ideation
Insights by: Pascal Pinck and Nadja Schnetzler

Pascal Pinck

Pascal Pinck is a strategic advisor and collaborator who helps organizations pursue high performance with a particular focus on Lean and Agile product development. He has worked with NASA, the U.S. Army, Raytheon, BASF, Kraft Foods, Media Temple, Vertafore, Inc., and many other organizations. He tweets at *@pascalpinck*.

Nadja Schnetzler

Nadja Schnetzler is one of the founders of the first Idea Factory in the world, BrainStore. Together with her husband Markus she is one of the pioneers in systematic idea and innovation management in Europe. After helping more than 500 companies from 5 continents to build their innovation management and to come up with better ideas, Nadja decided in 2012 to follow another passion of hers: She consults musicians, mainly in the area of Ancient Music, in areas of positioning, storytelling and communication. With her new venture, "Word and Deed", she thus combines her expertise in communication, journalism (her first education) and innovation.

Nadja uses Personal Kanban and the Pomodoro Technique in her individual projects and uses a mix of Agile techniques and practices for client projects with larger groups. Nadja is a mother of two children. In her two blogs "One Ocean Apart" and "Handsoffparenting" she talks about her liberal and unusual parenting beliefs and the less than orthodox life of her family.

▶   Kanban did exactly what it was supposed to ... And that was very scary."

   ~ Nadja Schnetzler

WHAT GOES UP ...

Markus Mettler and Nadja Schnetzler founded BrainStore in 1989 when they saw how many people were struggling with the innovation process. From companies struggling to figure out the complexities of entering a new market with their product, to the seemingly simple challenge of a family wondering how they could turn a milestone birthday into a memorable event for a grandparent.

The company invented the Idea Machine, a structured methodology that could help individuals and companies understand and cultivate breakthrough ideas and set up systematic processes to turn these ideas into tangible results. Typically, projects were run at the customer site or remotely from BrainStore in collaboration with the client's staff.

The Idea Machine

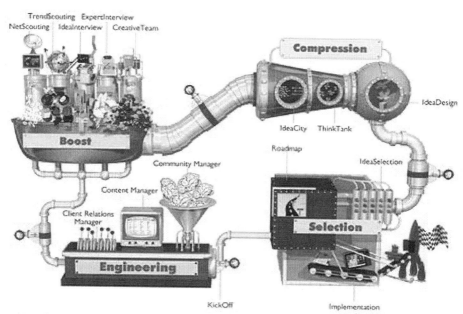

For a company selling a completely intangible product—the expertise to help people solve their own problems rather than an actual solution to a problem—BrainStore performed impressively and grew rapidly from a staff of 20 to 80 between 2004 and 2007.

... MUST GO DOWN

However, as so often happens, continued success and expansion brought its own set of challenges to the company. The internal work processes became increasingly involved and information—the lifeblood of a company specializing in knowledge work—no longer flowed easily within the company. Management drove and mandated a move to a more structured environment as they felt it was necessary to support the growing multitude of client projects.

By 2010, BrainStore wasn't doing that well anymore. The pressures of the global economic downturn had affected them

> **SCALING IS NOT DOING IT BIGGER**
>
> *A typical scaling strategy is to try and control and replicate identical behavior. While ultimately counterproductive, this is understandable – we've found something that works and we want to expand that success. As unscalable processes break down, we often mandate quick fixes rather than Kaizen approaches.*

severely, since far fewer companies were able or willing to make use of their services in uncertain financial conditions. This led management to implement stringent cost-cutting measures. They reduced the full-time workforce from 80 people the year before to a mere 30 permanent

SHRINK TO FIT?

Down-sizing is a common reaction in times of economic decline. The people who remain cannot do the same amount of work in the same way as before – but demands remain unchanged, leaving people overloaded. The low morale and fear generated by this "do the same with less" philosophy in turn create a spiraling cycle of waste and delay, sometimes with catastrophic results.

staff members who were soon struggling to manage the remaining workload effectively. Rather ironically, Suddenly, BrainStore's innovation experts found themselves facing many of the same challenges clients usually asked them to help solve.

The company was in trouble. Morale was low and more people were leaving, resulting in new hires who quickly noticed and echoed the low company morale. BrainStore urgently needed a different approach that would enable them to continue operating effectively without the former workforce and knowledge that was lost through rapid staff reduction and ongoing staff turnover.

THE DRIVE TO THRIVE INSTEAD OF SURVIVE

During 2010, the BrainStore leadership—Markus and Nadja—decided it was time to change their focus from cost-cutting to maximizing the company's revenue. The best defense is offense, right? Consequently, the sales team was charged with the enormous task of increasing revenue strongly in a tough market. Under great strain to deliver results, the team started showing signs of stress and their revenue growth initiatives were not having the desired results.

At this point, Pascal Pinck had started chatting to Nadja about the concepts of Agile and Lean process management. He had been working for BrainStore since 2008 as a consultant and facilitator, and had already begun to experiment with these methodologies at project-level. As staffing levels and budgets at BrainStore continued to drop, Pascal urged Nadja and the management team to consider applying these ideas to the company's activities as a whole.

Nadja found the principles of "inspect and adapt" and "continuous improvement" highly intriguing, as both were already inherent in the Idea Machine methodology and, to a lesser extent, in the BrainStore company culture. Post-completion project reviews (somewhat similar to retrospectives in Agile/Scrum parlance) were in fact already standard practice at the company.

Although Nadja was enthusiastic about experimenting with various Agile and Lean approaches with the sales team—where the need for immediate improvement was keenest—the members of the team were more cautious. Although they could see that there was good reason to try something new, they were skeptical and exhausted. They had all been feeling enormous pressure to deliver results, especially given the recent drop in revenue, and there had been a persistent feeling that—despite long hours—key priorities were slipping and some of the most valuable work was not actually getting done.

The team briefly experimented with Scrum, but found that it was not practical to manage ongoing sales cycles. Iterations didn't match the flow of work in consulting, where tasks and projects don't follow a preconceived plan. The backlog of work for the average "Brain" (the name that BrainStore employees used for themselves) needed to be more flexible. Seeing this disconnect, the team decided to migrate to a more flow-based system, using an unused whiteboard and paper to track their work-in-progress very visibly in their work area.

Within a few days of visually tracking their work, the morale in the sales team started lifting. The overwhelming workload up to that point had taken a severe mental toll. The team had been feeling out-of-touch, unresponsive, and unproductive. With the introduction of the visual control, they were able to actually see the work they were doing. They could measure their productivity in simple, yet real and effective ways. And as a team, they were actually starting to relate to each other and the work everybody was doing.

With this much-needed injection of positive energy in the organization, it wasn't long before employees in other teams became curious about what they were doing that was having such a positive effect. And as the members of the sales team were key players in the organization, their adoption of the the approach boded well for a wider implementation.

Or so BrainStore management thought.

GO BIG OR GO HOME

Two weeks later, based on the positive effect on the sales team, management tried another intervention. They unilaterally and unexpectedly dissolved all existing teams into two cross-functional teams with separate kanban-style visual controls for all work in progress. Each team had a Product Owner (called a "Champ"). Team members and management could add work to the shared backlog for the two teams, and the two Champs negotiated priorities and decided jointly which team would do the work.

Much to management's surprise, this blanket adoption of mandated Kanban did not have the positive impact they had envisioned. Whereas the sales team had agreed to try out the new approach, the other teams balked at having the change forced upon them. This was especially true in the case of teams that already had

ZEAL!

Nadja and Markus saw marked improvement with Kanban and wanted more. However, we see in the sales implementation some key words, like "experiment", "agreed" and "decided," that indicate that the sales team was thinking about how they worked and what would help them: successful Kaizen in action.

BrainStore's Management wanted to scale that success.

Unfortunately, the success had little to do with kanban and more to do with coherence; sales understood the changes and their relevance.

In their zeal to scale success, Nadja and Markus shocked the already fragile organization with confusing and abrupt change—the antithesis of Kaizen.

a strong self-organizational culture, and in cases where employees had strong emotional attachments to their specific (functional) roles.

A case in point was the operations team that ran the BrainStore client workshops. This team consisted of highly specialized members who previously operated with great flexibility and leeway. They now reported that they felt like cogs in a machine, simply executing the work that someone else had assigned to them.

Despite the strongly negative reception the change received from some people, some benefits were perceived by management:

⇨ Team members could no longer choose to work only on their specialist areas. Required to work on tasks unknown to them, they were forced to ask each other for help. This was facilitating rapid knowledge transfer among the remaining workforce.

⇨ Daily and weekly progress was clearly visible to all team members and to management.

⇨ The teams celebrated their successes and even indulged in some friendly competition between the two teams, which helped to diffuse some of the tension. There's nothing quite like comparing completed tasks and sharing a drink together in the backyard to keep things fun!

⇨ Some team members reported that it felt really good to move a work item to **Done**, especially when Done meant literally sticking a fork through it!

For a short while at least, these benefits outweighed the negatives. However, two clear camps—for and against this new way of working—had started to form around outspoken team members in the teams.

This was further compounded because Nadja—actively involved in and driving the Kanban implementation— and a new management hire often did not agree on how Kanban should be used in the business.

Within a few weeks, the internal conflict was at a boiling point. This atmosphere was not pleasant to work in—not for the teams and not for Nadja. Already under pressure with her workload as Champ, the resistance from the now very disgruntled teams was having a deeply personal and painful effect on her, pushing her to the brink of burnout.

It was abundantly clear to management that a serious intervention was needed to salvage the situation.

PUTTING PRINCIPLES AND PEOPLE FIRST?

Two months after BrainStore embarked on their Big Bang rollout, Nadja took four weeks emergency leave and the cross-functional teams were suspended. In Nadja's absence, the remaining leadership held a series of long meetings and discussions with the employees to expose all their concerns and frustrations about the work approach they were expected to follow.

The depth of unhappiness expressed by staff left management feeling that more fundamental changes were still needed. One of the key complaints from the teams was the fact that having Nadja as Champ was not working and was, in fact, creating a bottleneck. The company could not afford to have management be the bottleneck for the design and approval of changes to all workflows and protocols. Team members were crying out for the authority to make decisions and reformulate processes without incurring bureaucratic delays, even (or especially!) under conditions of uncertainty. But how, then, could the firm assure a high level of organizational learning and quality control?

Markus Mettler, BrainStore's CEO, decided that the company's future hinged on getting to the root of this problem. He and a core group of leaders went into isolation for about two weeks and emerged with what they saw as an effective and sustainable solution: *The BrainStore Code of Conduct* (see below). The Code was shared on Google Docs where people could examine it at their leisure, and was also presented to staff in a series of all-hands meetings by Markus.

> ## IT'S THE SYSTEM
>
> *Management and staff strike a precarious balance here. The "Champ" role – a Product Owner with Scrum Master overtones – led to a definable bottleneck. Unfortunately, Nadja as an individual was identified as the bottleneck, rather than the role she was playing in their process. The psychological term for this is Fundamental Attribution Error – Nadja and the situation became synonymous.*

> ### HERE'S YOUR NEW CODE OF CONDUCT!
>
> *This is the full text of Brainstore's Code of Conduct. Note as you read through it that the text, while open to comment, was drawn up largely be cribbing work from others and not speaking in a voice authentic to or written by the angry and distressed "Brains."*
>
> *This is a "best practice"*

THE BRAINSTORE "CODE OF CONDUCT"

What is Agile and why do we use it?

The basis of our way of working are the code of conduct and our purpose:

⇨ We will reliably **delight customers** by giving them access to the Idea Machine and having fun while doing it.

⇨ We will **optimize the performance of the organization** as a whole.

⇨ We will constantly **improve value flow, personal satisfaction, and team performance.**

Working Agile means respecting the following principles.[1]

We are uncovering better ways of developing products by doing it and helping others do it.

We have come to value:

---

[1]   *"Agile Manifesto" - http://Agilemanifesto.org/*

⇨ Individuals and interactions over processes and tools

⇨ Working products over perfection

⇨ Customer collaboration over contract negotiation

⇨ Responding to change over following a plan

While there is value in both, we value the items on the left more.

What does Agile mean for me?

Working Agile means **changing many habits**. It means **working as a true team** (not just working together in a team), **being very open with each other** and **trying to become better as a team** all the time. It also means taking on different roles depending on what the organization needs most at the time. Most of all, it means that everyone is working together and working with the client to **delight the client**.

The roles in our Agile process

1. Champ:

Help the team deliver exceptional customer value in environments of high uncertainty by:

⇨ Advocating for spoken and unspoken desires and needs of the customer

⇨ Maintaining and prioritizing the backlog that serves those customers

⇨ Promoting constant exchange of relevant information between team and customers

2. Team Member:

I will take my share in delivering exceptional customer value and help my team to achieve personal satisfaction.

3. Facilitator (one of the team members, in large projects also as an exclusive role):

Help the team move towards higher performance and greater personal satisfaction by:

⇨ Helping the team to discover barriers and help the team to remove them

⇨ Promoting constant exchange of relevant information between team members

⇨ Helping the team to have higher quality conversations

⇨ Helping the team to optimally deal with time, resources and scope based on the allocated resources per backlog item

⇨ Helping the team to decide on when and how to exchange information, including stand up meetings and retrospectives

Notes on the Facilitator Role

In each work cycle, the team decides who in the team takes on the role of the facilitator.

Each person at BrainStore (also trainees and freelancers) can take on all three roles.

Work Organization

We work in cycles (work units) with durations of four hours up to several weeks. Each cycle is initiated by a Champ and has a number of Team Members. One person of the team is assuming the role of the Facilitator.

<End of Code of Conduct>

FROM PAN TO FIRE

However bad things seemed to be before the code was presented, that picture paled in comparison to what happened next.

Most employees were shocked at the minimalistic work organization as proposed by management. Many also did not see how a lofty set of principles could even begin to address the interpersonal and organizational conflict they were experiencing. Some team members also felt that this approach could not possibly represent a credible solution to the company's financial woes. **Within a week, half of the BrainStore team had stopped coming to work.**

> ### LET THEM EAT CODE
>
> *Enforced process change – even if we call it Agile, Lean, or Kanban – is still enforced process change. It is antithetical to Agile and Lean ideals. It is process over people.*

Management (without Nadja, who was still on leave) convened an urgent meeting to clarify the application of the code of conduct. They realized, in hindsight, that creating and presenting the code on their own, without staff involvement and without providing context, had resulted in what could only be described as mutiny.

Unsurprisingly, tensions were high and the meeting started out in explosive fashion with arguments and blame. Considerable damage had already been done by the economic uncertainty of the company combined with a haphazard, unilateral, and poorly communicated process shift. As the meeting progressed, some of the team began to accept that management had good intentions, and also noted that staff members could immediately alter and improve their own processes in the future.

However, a lot of suspicion remained. The BrainStore culture had been damaged, potentially irrevocably; by the way management had dealt with the process changes to date, resulting in a low-trust environment. Only a handful of people left the meeting satisfied. The initial changes to their work processes had been all about the mechanics of implementing a kanban board with associated metrics, rather than finding an optimal, yet flexible work structure that would reflect their *organizational goals and culture*. The changes had also fundamentally disempowered team members, rather than enabling them to actively manage and control their work environment.

GETTING BACK TO BUSINESS

Unhappily for BrainStore, many of the skeptical employees left the company. The few remaining employees set to implementing the new approach nervously, but with hope. Markus ran an initial series of two to four hour cycles to help people adapt to the new approach. The extremely short cycles enabled them to inspect and adapt based on lessons learned very rapidly, rather than allow the teams to devolve into demotivation, as with the initial attempt to enforce use of the kanban.

Nadja returned to work as the teams were already actively implementing the principles from the Code of Conduct. Her initial reaction was that management had taken an extreme approach in her absence—and one with which she certainly was not happy.

It didn't take her long to see however, that the surviving employees were significantly happier and relishing the opportunity to contribute in teams where they felt they could add most value based on their expertise. The self-organizing work cycles were a tangible way of valuing individuals and interactions ahead of tools and processes, and people were responding positively to being valued and appreciated in this way. Team members also spoke frankly about the benefits of the regular end-of-cycle reviews, which allowed them to obtain feedback from the product and project "visionaries" much more frequently and reliably.

Upon reflection, Nadja realized that her absence had made it possible for the teams to start crafting their own lightweight and flexible approach, instead of blindly following an approach invented and enforced by somebody else. That didn't make them self-organization experts overnight, though.

BEYOND AGILE

It took them about two to three quarters to apply the cycle approach as the standard for all projects at BrainStore. Champs evolved to launching projects on an ongoing basis with employees subscribing to the cycles they want to participate in ten days in advance. Specialized roles for customer projects were eliminated for the most part, with only a small core team remaining in very defined support roles such as IT infrastructure and financial management.

Instead of enforcing the Kanban as a method, teams could choose to use a kanban board to track the work on a specific project. They could also choose any other tracking or visualization mechanism that served their purpose.

REFLECTING ON THE JOURNEY

Nadja reflects on the process evolution at BrainStore and shares some of her feelings about their journey:

"I don't regret this journey. Although I felt less in control of things at BrainStore, I realized that that was a good thing for the organization and for me. It is never good for one person to control everything. With Champs sharing ownership of the work, the pressure of accountability was spread throughout the organization. Knowledge was spread throughout the organization. People felt empowered and we all felt more productive. We knew what's happening without feeling overwhelmed. I for one, felt a lot calmer."

She recognizes that they could have approached things differently. It would have been better to give individual teams the choice to adopt Kanban themselves, allowing the change to expand organically throughout the organization. They could also have established work policies upfront through discussion and agreement, rather than starting with a brute force implementation of the Code that eventually led to an employee revolt.

Nadja continues:

"We tried to be too revolutionary. We wanted to embrace Lean principles to reduce waste and Work-in-Progress, but we didn't realize how enforcing our vision without involving our teams in this radical change would damage the fabric of BrainStore. We had to learn that the hard way."

CODA

BrainStore was declared bankrupt in December 2011. Markus and Nadja have learned much during the BrainStore experience and are continuing with their business idea based on what they learned. Visit www.gotomorrow.com for more details on Markus and Nadja's new venture.

TAMING UNCERTAINTY IN THE MEDIA INDUSTRY
CCRTV Achieves Flow with Metrics

VITAL STATISTICS

Company: CCRTV Interactive/CCMA Information Systems
Location: Barcelona, Spain
Industry and Domain: Software development, host connectivity systems and security management for the broadcast television industry
Insights by: Ángel Medinilla

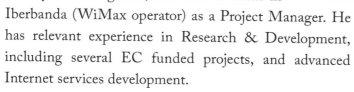

Ángel Medinilla has more than 14 years working experience in the ICT market—five of them in AUNA (second biggest Telco operator in Spain) as a Project Manager and Systems Engineer, and two of them in Iberbanda (WiMax operator) as a Project Manager. He has relevant experience in Research & Development, including several EC funded projects, and advanced Internet services development.

His contributions to the Agile community include several presentations on Slideshare, two blogs (Spanish / English), the official translation to Spanish of the Agile Manifesto, the translation of Henrik Kniberg's *"Scrum and XP from the Trenches,"* and the coordination of the translation of Kniberg and Skarin's *"Kanban vs. Scrum."*

SUMMARY

The study covers the period between April and November 2010. At the time, CCRTV Interactive had approximately 11 teams, each with an average of eight team members. The teams were mainly collocated or scattered across the same building. However, most teams rely strongly on external suppliers, resulting in a high degree of external dependencies. In some cases, suppliers from remote offices even served as virtual members of the development teams based in Barcelona.

In April 2010, the nature of the existing Scrum implementation in the media-related software products was challenged when the Product Owners were asked to freeze the project scope for a full sprint; in other words, add no unplanned work to the sprint at all. This was because daily urgent, unplanned requests, e.g. production bugs and immediate commercial requirements, were negatively impacting the team's velocity, motivation and productivity—typical side-effects of constant context-switching.

As CCRTV services the fast-changing broadcast television industry, it would have been all but impossible to completely remove such last-minute scope changes from the environment. Conversely, the development teams were concerned that a full Kanban implementation would shift their focus completely to urgent short-term needs prioritized by business customers, thus losing sight of important long-term projects and the company's strategic commitment. As a result, a tailor-made Agile/Lean implementation emerged as a successful way to provide a balance between the uncertainties of ever-changing scope by helping the teams to understand their value stream and the nature of their work, while still maintaining momentum on the company's medium and long-term commitments.

BACKGROUND

Catalonian TV (TV3) employs roughly 2,700 people and operates both TV and radio stations for a population of 7.4 million people in the autonomous Spanish community of Catalonia. Their IT operations are divided across two main areas: CCRTV Interactive takes care of the New Media strategy, including community portals, web sites and mobile services, while CCMA Information Systems Area (CCMA ISA) operates the IT infrastructure for the whole group, including operational TV back office infrastructure. Their main client is the internal organization, although they also assist external customers on projects such as media campaigns or other regional television channels that use the CCMA ISA back office and TV infrastructure products.

CCRTV operates as an independent company within the TV group, while CCMA ISA is a more traditional IT functional area inside the parent company.

The media environment results in a very reactive culture inside the company, with predictability seemingly impossible to achieve and management sometimes resorting to merely managing the daily uncertainty as an operational strategy. In addition, having an internal client-supplier relationship tended to introduce a lack of disciplined and structured development processes, thus affecting the ability of the development teams to adequately deliver results to match the demand. These two factors led to teams being overwhelmed by high levels of context-switching against the backdrop of poorly defined development priorities and no real insight into the actual workload or output of the teams. This had led to a number of missed project deadlines, and was impacting the ability of CCRTV Interactive to provide quality service to the rest of the organization.

Early in 2010, senior management agreed to provide Agile training to the entire CCRTV Interactive company. This initiative was spurred on by a handful of technical managers in CCRTV Interactive who had been actively learning about Agile methods and the extensive Scrum and Kanban input provided by a former BBC New Media employee now working at CCRTV Interactive. This was followed by a kick-off implementation in the second quarter of 2010, with on-going coaching and further project implementations, also at CCM ISA, as early results were very promising.

STARTING WITH AGILE

The starting point for the initial Agile implementation was a vanilla implementation of Scrum at CCRTV interactive. The typical elements of Scrum were put in place within about four weeks, generally with enthusiasm and support from team members:

⇨ Cross-functional teams (initially six teams of eight people each) were created with graphic designers, developers, architects, and all other skills needed to successfully build functionality incrementally in time boxes.

⇨ Scrum Masters were identified from within the teams, and the role of the technical project manager, who previously analyzed work, proposed the best way to do it, and divided tasks amongst team members, was scrapped in favor of team self-organization. In some cases, the former project managers became internal experts the team could rely on for technical input.

⇨ Team retrospectives produced impediment backlogs to be worked on by team members, line managers and Scrum Masters.

⇨ Mandatory daily meetings took place on every team, and if some members were outside the building, video-conferencing tools were used to ensure maximum participation.

⇨ A Product Owner was appointed for every team to manage the backlog and participate in sprint planning and review activities with the teams.

MANAGING WORK DEPENDENCIES OUTSIDE THE TEAM

One of the immediate challenges in this implementation was how to deal effectively with external work dependencies between the Content Department and the Scrum teams.

At CCRTV, Product Owners were appointed within the Content Department, seen as the internal proxy of the client to the teams. However, the Content team members were not part of the Scrum teams. Although the coaches recommended including the Content crew as team members, this was not practical. Not only did the Content staff also have other daily tasks outside of the sprint work, they were also managed by a different manager.

Several discussions on this topic led to a possible solution. Tasks that were supposed to be done or unblocked by the Content team—a large department, separate from the Scrum teams—were shown on the Scrum team's physical board. Members of the Content team attended daily Scrums and reported on their assignments by the team. Using this simple visual control and feedback mechanism helped to shift everyone's attitude. The Scrum teams no longer felt that they worked for Content, and that, since both the Content and Scrum teams needed the projects to end successfully, having the Content teams help them remove impediments and work on items assigned by the team would be in everybody's interest.

Another part of the working relationship challenge related to the role of the Product Owners. In some cases where teams took care of several projects at once, it was not possible to have a single Product Owner. The teams found themselves dealing with two or even three Product Owners in a single sprint.

This was seen as an impediment for the teams. To address this, Master Product Owners were identified from within the Content Department to ensure that there would be a single sprint backlog for every team at the beginning of every sprint.

> **DO IT HARDER AGAIN**
>
> *Again the now common anti-pattern of finding waste and trying to curb it by adding more of the same rears its head. Product Owners were not working, so CCRTV added more (Master) Product Owners.*

The Master Product Owner plays the traditional Scrum Product Owner role of prioritizing the product backlog, while the individual Product Owners help the Master Product Owner to write stories and validate them at the sprint review. A single Master Product Owner usually has to take care of two teams. Overlapping two-week team sprints were designed to ensure that the Master Product Owner could attend one sprint Planning and one sprint Review every week. On week one, team one would start a sprint and the Master Product Owner would attend Team One's sprint planning, while on week two he would attend Team Two's sprint planning. The same cadence applies to the sprint review for the two teams.

KEEPING WORK VISIBLE

Each team kept a single backlog with stories for different products and projects represented in the backlog. This backlog was managed in an issue tracker tool (Jira) and sometimes in Excel spreadsheets, but the use of physical boards in each team was strongly encouraged. Some teams saw this as a source of duplicate effort at first, but they soon learned to enjoy their physical boards for the tangible benefits when a physical board was introduced.

The physical boards allow for a higher degree of inter-activity during the daily Scrum meetings or when dis-cussing sprint scope with the Product Owner, especially compared to using an Excel spreadsheet projected on a wall while the Product Owner or the Scrum Master has the only keyboard and mouse access.

But probably the most important benefit of a physical task board is that it functions as a "Team Totem." It sup-ports and enforces the vision of the team as a tribe, as something above the individual contribution of any team member. The role the boards play in team identity became a spe-cific reason not to standardize the task boards across teams: a lack of com-mon structure and some loss of board legibility by people outside the team is preferable to the loss of team identity. Scrum Masters and line manag-ers should empower teams to evolve their board design to reflect team identity, structure and specific value stream.

TEAM TOTEM

With BrainStore, we saw that the appearance of a kanban board is meaningless if it isn't serving the team. For CCRTV, however, the board was simultaneously providing the team with needed information (value for the team) and guiding the team forward (value for the organization).

Of course the physical task boards also function as infor-mation radiators where managers and other stakehold-ers can see relevant data about teams and their projects.

Boards can reflect team roles, names, structure, projects, goals, impediments, schedule, and the time and date of the next sprint Demo. Although this information can as easily reside on a wiki or in an issue tracker, people are less likely to access this information regularly. Information radiators make this data visible to everyone 24-7, thus improving communication, knowledge transfer and providing greater visibility to issues.

MANAGING VARIABLE WORKLOAD FROM MULTIPLE WORK STREAMS

At CCRTV, there is always a high degree of uncertainty about sprint scope. The news world is highly reactive to external events—events out of the control of either the team or the Product Owner. In addition, teams are not only required to develop new products. They also have daily operational responsibilities that often vary.

Context-switching was therefore considered an unavoidable part of life in the media environment that the teams had to deal with effectively. The teams experimented with a number of approaches within the Scrum context until CCRTV hit upon Scrumban as a sustainable mechanism to deal with variability.

> **VARIATION**
>
> *CCRTV is actively experimenting to adapt to variation in their workflow. Rather than hiding from interruptions, or trying to legislate them away, their experiments all deal with understanding the variation and adapting.*

TALES OF CONTINUOUS IMPROVEMENT

Divide and Conquer

One of the experiments was the creation of a separate operations and maintenance team. Although this did serve to contain the variability to specific teams, it had a number of negative side-effects and the experiment was suspended after a few sprints. The teams started feeling disconnected from each other, with knowledge becoming scattered and divided across the teams. Team morale was also noticeably lower on those teams who were not assigned to develop new products and were only fighting fires. Cross-dependencies with other teams also complicated the ability of these teams to work effectively in isolation.

Head in the Sand

Another approach was to not even try to plan for uncertainty. Anything that came up during sprint and that was not in the original sprint backlog scope, was considered "out of scope" and simply logged as impediments. This approach led to a lack of understanding of what was really happening in the Scrum teams during sprints and it made it harder to predict sprint velocity and outcomes. As a result, CCRTV lost sight of small tasks that added real value to customers that were not reflected as part of sprint velocity.

Shorter Sprints

The teams also experimented with sprint length. At one point, sprints were reduced to one week. This was good for some teams, but in the majority of cases, clients were not available every week. Although lack of client availability was reported as an impediment, addressing it was not a simple matter. Meeting with a client proxy (Product Owner) on a daily basis worked well, but introduced a proxy-client feedback that caused the Product Owner to introduce fixes, requirements and priority changes or even new urgent stories in the middle of the sprint once the client was finally able to evaluate the delivered stories.

INTRODUCING A BUFFER TO MANAGE UNCERTAINTY

Finally, instead of treating variable operational needs as a separate problem, a certain amount of capacity in each team's sprint capacity was allocated to deal with urgent needs, sudden priorities and "unknown unknowns."

This average capacity was initially benchmarked by designating an area of the team board to uncertainty in a so-called buffer value stream. The existing Scrum work remained on the top half of the physical board to visually enforce the idea that, while uncertainty exists and should be managed and may sometimes even be of higher priority than the Scrum backlog, the Scrum backlog is still the long-term top priority. Having the buffer items visible separately from the planned work, made it possible to track how much time the team was spending on unplanned work, thereby establishing a baseline for average Buffer capacity.

Scrum

Pending	Selected.	Dev.	Valid.	Integration	Done!

Buffer

Pending	Selected.	Dev.	Valid.	Integration	Done!

Kanban board with Scrum & buffer space concept

It soon became clear that the new buffer space introduced a prioritization issue. Should a team member start a Scrum task next or should he take care of new buffer stories? The buffer space also acted as a "happy hour" call for Product Owners, and some of them started creating all their new requests in the buffer instead of in the Scrum section of the board.

To solve the prioritization issues and enforce some sort of control on buffer usage, three qualities of service and a velocity limit were put in place for the buffer. The three qualities of service[1] were defined explicitly as follows:

⇨ **FIRE:** Drop whatever you are doing right now and take care of this issue. We understand this leads to context-switching and affects team veloc-

---

1   *Capacity reservation and prioritization mechanisms that allow certain classes of services to be granted specific service levels: for example, shorter response time or higher prioritization.*

ity, but this is a high risk and needs to be solved even if it leads to poorer sprint results. Every fire request will be severely audited at the end of the sprint and should be part of an intensive root cause analysis exercise in the team retrospective so that action plans can be put in place that will prevent this kind of fire to happen ever again.

⇨ **PRIO:** This is high priority, so when you finish what you are doing right now, neatly close it down and open this new task instead of another Scrum or ASAP task. Context-switching happens, but in a less hurtful manner. Product Owners have a set goal to reduce PRIO stories at the end of the sprint, and the company has even designed a "Best Product Owner" award for the Product Owner who keeps his FIRE and PRIO statistics lower than the others. This friendly internal contest is also tracked visually, enforcing peer review amongst the Product Owners.

⇨ **ASAP:** These stories should be attended to as soon as we have some buffer space available. If there's no buffer space—Scrum stories are more important. If the Product Owner would like to sacrifice the sprint goal in favor of this story, he should re-prioritize it to PRIO.

Buffer space was measured using a burn-down chart against a proposed buffer load. For example, if a team capable of doing 100 story points over a sprint decides to spare 20% of their resources to manage uncertainty, 20 points on their sprint burn-down track every task or full story allocated to buffer time. When the buffer burn-down hits zero, it means that the team is out of capacity for uncertainty management, and any other tasks allocated to buffer work will very probably impact the sprint goal. For accuracy, buffer tasks are only estimated after they are completed.

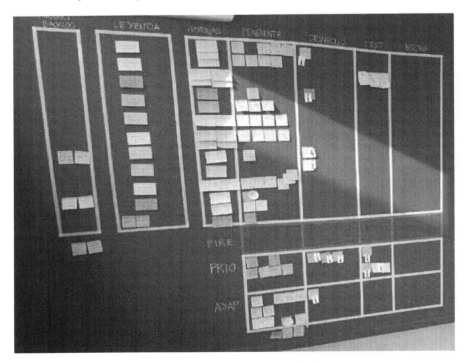

Wall Kanban with Scrum and buffer lane with Quality of Service

USING THE BUFFER TO THROTTLE OR INCREASE CAPACITY

Over time, additional practices evolved around the use of the buffer. These practices enabled the teams to adapt their capacity for new work dynamically based on current business priorities.

If a Scrum project deadline was near and it seemed hard to meet, the Product Owner could cancel the buffer allocation for a sprint and the team would immediately obtain a +20% Scrum velocity. The teams called this "Turbine Boost." This would of course be at the cost of decreasing velocity after the deadline because the team would need to attend to all the buffer calls that couldn't be addressed before the deadline. Boosting the system like this would usually also incur some measure of technical debt and was not encouraged.

Another practice was to allow for the dynamic reallocation of Scrum work capacity during the sprint. For example, based on historical evidence after a few sprints, some teams committed to 80 story points and 120 buffer man hours for each sprint. If more buffer hours were needed by the Product Owner for FIRE, PRIO, and ASAP stories that were introduced during the sprint, then the 80 expected Scrum story points would start to decrease, allowing for an increase in buffer man hours.

To enable rapid and informed Product Owner decisions based on sprint status, buffer usage, and sprint goal statistics were communicated on a daily basis during the daily Scrum.

METRICS

Explicitly limiting Work-in-Progress (WIP) is usually a key component of successfully implementing Kanban. However, as the CCRTV teams were very new to Agile, they found it difficult to commit to hard and fast WIP

BEYOND AGILE

limits on every board column for the buffer. Even limits based on quality of service were not considered an option. For example, the Content teams could not lower the number of FIRE items in progress concurrently, since they had little decision-making power over the number and frequency of client requests.

Initially, the teams therefore opted for soft cross-board WIP limits that were enforced through the use of personal avatars. Far from being something trivial or funny—fun also being very important for an Agile team—personal avatars played into the personal customization of the board by the team. They also dramatically improve visibility of what each team member is working on at any given moment.

WHAT MAKES A GOOD METRIC

When CCRTV looked for metrics and ways to limit their WIP, they came to an interesting conclusion: avatars could be both a metric and a WIP limiting device. Not only were the avatars themselves limited, but they are also a metric for individual team members to know they are becoming overloaded. If you look at the board and see yourself on too many tickets, you know (along with everyone else) that you have too much to do.

At CCRTV, every team member has only two or three avatars representing themselves, so they shouldn't be working on more than three tasks at the same time. If there are tasks on the board without an avatar, that could mean they are blocked or that whoever owns them has started too many tasks. Tasks without avatars generate conversation during daily Scrum meetings and are an opportunity for team members to help each other and to improve the work process in some way.

MORE METRICS

As they fine-tuned their approach, the teams introduced new metrics. They found that the buffer was being used for two types of work: small, new unpredictable items demanded by the customer (*value*), as well as bug fixes and re-work (*waste*). The teams started representing these two very different types of work with different card colors. The velocity for each type is tracked separately in two measurements they call "Good Karma" and "Bad Karma." Good Karma represents value being constantly delivered to the customer, while Bad Karma keeps the team from delivering more value.

> **CHOOSING A METRIC**
>
> *You can quantify something subjective, like fun, karma, and happiness. The important thing is to make sure that the relative scale reflects proportionally what you deem as important.*

These two measures make it possible to identify trends in the team's productivity as well as the quality of work that is being delivered. In the image below, a significant increase in Bad Karma is going to lead directly to a drop in Good Karma. Understanding these trends enables the Product Owner and the team to make better day-to-day decisions when choosing buffer tasks.

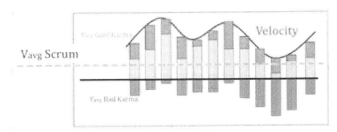

Better predictability through better understanding of average velocity components

The teams have also started using typical Kanban measurements like Cycle Time and Lead Time. Cycle Time and Lead Time are being tracked quite simply by writing down the task introduction date, task start date and task completion date.

Cycle Time has helped the teams to better modulate the size of tasks, as they can highlight tasks to the Product Owners that required a longer cycle time ("outliers") and suggest ways that the task could have been split to produce more averaged-sized tasks. If splitting the task in future would not be possible, the team now records the nature of the task to help flag potential outliers in the future.

Lead Time has been used to produce forecasts and estimates on delivery dates and buffer completion dates when the buffer backlog grew too much. Electronic tools allowed the production of histograms and other statistical data that could be discussed in Product Owner and Scrum Master meetings. This information allowed the Product Owners to better define and manage their stories and tasks, while providing more predictability for the process as a whole through better backlog grooming.

The teams also experimented with Cumulative Flow Diagrams (CFDs), but found that they did not provide any more information than already obtained with the previously described metrics and graphics. In the spirit of "Inspect and Adapt", the teams discontinued the creation of CFDs as a wasteful practice.

THE IMPORTANCE OF KEEPING UNCERTAINTY UNDER CONTROL

Implementing a Kanban-style buffer at CCRTV has highlighted some key psychological aspects of using a Scrumban approach that puts an emphasis on visibility and tracking real work in a highly unpredictable environment.

This kind of approach certainly provides a greater feeling of safety for both the teams and the Product Owners. If an expedite request should come along, the teams have some tolerance to accommodate it without feeling overwhelmed. It also prevents the teams from being blamed for poor velocity when they are in fact attending to mandatory requirements, as all work is tracked either through the sprint velocity or the buffer statistics.

However, even with better uncertainty management, team morale suffers when too much uncertainty is added to a sprint. Even when a Product Owner calls for a "100% buffer" sprint—to attend to an urgent ad hoc project or to invest in technical debt reduction—and the team is not held accountable for low sprint velocity, morale drops.

BEYOND AGILE

Teams like to advance. They like to add value by building new things. And they like to maintain a high level of productivity. Yes, Agile tell us to embrace change, but unconstrained change destroys the advantages of being adaptable due to the loss of purpose and direction. The coaches at Proyectalis believed that people expect some predictability and were not yet ready for an entirely chaotic world of daily prioritization.

Interestingly, one of the greatest wins of this approach has been the improvement in the relationship between the Product Owner and the CCRTV / CCMA teams. Before the introduction of the buffer, it caused Product Owners a lot of stress if teams were not working on the Scrum backlog because they could not see what value the team was adding. Now, it's clear to most Product Owners that a team working on PRIO tasks is indeed contributing, even if the sprint velocity has decreased. There are the odd cases where a Product Owner might still insist that his team must achieve both the sprint commitment and close every ticket opened on the Buffer board, but even in these cases the teams now have enough upfront information on the Product Owner's average buffer demand so that they can decrease their commitment accordingly.

CONCLUSION

In a highly unpredictable environment as the one described, the Scrumban approach improved visibility and flexibility, created better understanding of what was happening during sprints, ensured closer client-supplier integration and lowered stress levels for everybody, on top of improving the relationship between the teams and Product Owners.

Adapting to the Scrumban approach required virtually no effort from the existing Scrum team, rather than dissolving the whole Scrum liturgy and expecting the team to spontaneously start improving their value stream with the only rule of keeping WIP low. Departing from a Scrum process, the team slowly transformed into a Lean and Kanban process by first limiting their WIP. However, this mixed model has now provided a very solid base from where the teams could switch to a full Kanban pull system somewhere in the future, when they realize that the "Scrum" lane is nothing other than a different class of service on a kanban board and that they could add stories to the lane on a daily basis instead of during a planned session at the start of every sprint.

SHIFTING TO COLLECTIVE OWNERSHIP OF QUALITY
Fifty-One's Scrumban Journey

TALES OF CONTINUOUS IMPROVEMENT

VITAL STATISTICS

Company: FiftyOne

Location: Tel Aviv, Israel

Industry and Domain: Software development, e-commerce

Insights by: Yuval Yeret and Ben Peer

Yuval Yeret

Yuval is leading the Kanban/Flow practice in AgileSparks, an international Lean/Agile consulting company. He has been in the technology management world since 1994. He graduated top of class from the IDF Mamram Computer School and in the last 17 years held various management positions in IT and Product Development including several Vice President of Research and Development positions, with a focus on the Networking and Storage worlds. Six years ago Yuval started used Lean/Agile thinking and practices to turn around technology organizations. On top of being a kanban guru and nominee for the 2011 Lean SSC Brickell Key Award, Yuval is also a seasoned Scrum practitioner and CSM/CSP/CSPO. Yuval is a big believer in pragmatic best-of-breed solution design, taking the best from each approach and not sticking to any particular dogma. Yuval is based in Israel, but you can often find him speaking, training and consulting in Europe and across the Atlantic.

Ben Peer

Ben Peer joined FiftyOne in 2000 and has more than fifteen years experience in the development of new technologies. As Senior Vice President of Technology, Ben has responsibility for all technological aspects of the FiftyOne solution as well as for the company's global operations. Among his key responsibilities are designing and evolving the underlying architecture of the FiftyOne solution, managing research and development globally, defining software interfaces for integration with strategic third parties, and helping orchestrate all of the company's product development initiatives.

Prior to joining FiftyOne, Ben co-founded SiteCore, an Internet start-up company, serving as the company's Chief Technology Officer. Earlier in his career, he led a product development team in Vcon, a developer and manufacturer of video-over-IP solutions. During his military service in the IDF, he developed software for the intelligence and communication forces.

Ben holds a B.Sc. in Mathematics and Computer Science from Ben-Gurion University.

BACKGROUND

FiftyOne Engineering, located in Tel Aviv, Israel, develops and maintains an online e-commerce system providing US-based retailers with the ability to extend their services internationally.

The main work products of the engineering team include:

⇨ New roadmap features aimed at increasing market reach and profitability of the system

⇨ Features aimed at improving customer success

⇨ Addressing escalated support cases that either required operational intervention or actual defect-fixing and patch deployment

Prior to adopting Agile, the FiftyOne team was using a waterfall-like process involving months-long releases, upfront design stages, and lengthy and painful testing phases—despite having considerable automated testing coverage at the system level. All of these conditions highlight the sub-optimal effectiveness of that process.

The engineering organization was comprised of three main technical teams:

⇨ Back-end/Server Team (3 people)

⇨ Front-end/Application Team (3 people)

⇨ Testing Team (4 people)

Each team had a team lead managing the people on the team and serving as the resident subject matter expert on the team's competency. Team leads reported to the Senior

Vice President in charge of Engineering (Ben Peer) who had experience with Extreme Programming (XP). He was also in charge of IT and Tech Support, and served on FiftyOne's overall management team. The entire Engineering team occupied a single space in Tel Aviv.

Product Management was led by the Vice President of Product (Paul), located on the west coast of the United States. A new Product Manager (Roman) with classic Scrum experience was hired just prior to FiftyOne's lean transition and was located on the east coast.

SETTING THE STAGE FOR CHANGE

When Ben approached the AgileSparks consultancy, they were looking for a major revolution in the operation of their Engineering department. They felt that something was drastically wrong with the current methodology, and together with fresh thinking brought in by a new Product Management Team, the time was ripe for a big J-curve improvement.

Based on the team's particular challenges and appetite for change, Scrum appeared to be an appropriate option to provide new ways of working within a new framework. It would also be a way to introduce and establish agile thinking as a whole in the Engineering department.

AgileSparks initiated the change process by discussing the overall engineering process with the FiftyOne management team and mapping the Scrum processes and roles to the current organization. The product team was assigned to the role of Product Owners. Instead of three separate teams, there were two feature teams with matching application, server and testing capabilities formed. One of the former team leads was assigned the role of Scrum Master for both teams, with the clear purpose of being a facilitator, not a project manager or team lead of any kind.

The department decided to start with two-week sprints. Each sprint was to include two days of code freeze and regression testing, followed by a deployment to a staging environment where changes can be previewed by stakeholders such as professional services, customer success, and preferred partners. One week after deployment to staging, the sprint deliverable would be deployed to production if no showstoppers were found in staging.

To support this team structure, stories had to change from being technical component-specific task-like stories to being actual feature and function stories. Significant cooperation and understanding was required from the product team to ensure a smooth transition in this regard. One of their fears was that changing to end-to-end stories would mean longer feedback cycles—they wanted to see something out of development after two to three days of work. They agreed, however, that seeing something at a real story level was much better than seeing a task and agreed to work with the team to slice stories to the right level to ensure a short feedback cycle.

READY, SET, SPRINT!

A few weeks into the engagement, the entire team participated in a two-day Scrum Team Workshop. The focus of the workshop was to open team members to the agile mindset and to expose them to the Scrum framework. This workshop established the foundation for ongoing coaching at FiftyOne.

The teams started sprinting immediately after the workshop. Armed with enough stories to get started, the AgileSparks consultants conducted the first Sprint planning and the teams committed to their sprint work and started working, with daily standups for each team.

From the outset, the product team introduced a kanban-based board to track stories through the development process. The board was modified slightly to incorporate the Scrum "sprint" concept by adding a sprint backlog. Apart from that, the team used the board more or less as is in AgileZen, an electronic kanban tool. With a distributed team, using an electronic board was the most feasible option.

TO TASK-BOARD OR NOT TO TASK-BOARD

One of the main questions the team struggled with when designing their initial board and process was whether they needed a task board in addition to the storyboard. The advantage of this is of course task-level visibility for team members. On the other hand, it would be another board to maintain.

They decided to delay the introduction of a task until it was really necessary. Lucky enough, by the time the team actually started sprinting, it became possible to track tasks on each card in AgileZen, so the team started using that as a light-weight way to track tasks, instead of having a separate task board. They continue to use this approach.

For Yuval Yeret from AgileSparks, this lighter approach reflects a trend:

"In general, we see more and more teams—even pure Scrum teams (...)—explore reducing the emphasis on tasks, moving from estimated tasks to enumerating tasks to getting rid of tasks, and moving to small fast-flowing stories. This has the benefit of reducing the overhead, saving time in planning meetings, and reducing opportunities for Parkinson's law and Student Syndrome. With tasks not estimated, the work doesn't expand to fill any container. On the other hand, without a clear goal, the sense of urgency can wane."

DEALING WITH REMOTE PRODUCT OWNERS

One of the first challenges that surfaced when starting sprints and daily meetings was the difficulty of communicating with very remote Product Owners. The time zone difference made it extremely difficult to engage the Product Owners in daily Scrum meetings and for them to answer requirements questions for the teams within an acceptable turnaround time. This was affecting the team's ability to deliver stories within their sprint commitment.

The solution that everyone agreed to try was to create a local Product Owner proxy. One of the team leads was assigned to this role. He would work with the product team and represent them when short cycle time was required. The Product team would still review story demos and accept them, and provide final decision authority on significant issues. But the aim was to resolve the majority of queries and issues locally.

In addition, the team started a daily Scrum of Scrums meeting. This meeting primarily focused on coordinating between the Scrum teams and the Product team overseas, specifically the East Coast Product Manager who was the main contact for the teams on most stories. Getting the Scrum teams to engage in this meeting was somewhat of a challenge, though. They expected the team leads to facilitate this, and didn't really see how their participation added value. Over time, however, the meeting did help to establish more direct contact between team members and the Product team.

TO COMMIT OR NOT TO COMMIT

Another early frustration felt by the team was the length of the Planning Game. After monitoring a few sprints, it became apparent that one of the key factors in the length of the Planning Game was the fact that a fixed commitment was expected. Although the stories were estimated using story points and planning poker, it was hard for the team to provide this level of commitment without diving into the details of a story.

On top of that, it seemed that the interaction around commitment was also having its effects on actual velocity, which turned out to be similar to the commitment, even if commitment was made at a very safe level. It became clear that commitment was holding an energized team back, rather than propelling them forward. The Engineering group started raising more and more questions about the need for a sprint-level commitment, especially since there was no real external driver behind the commitment.

Observing this, Yuval suggested to the team that they do away with the sprint-level commitment and try a new model: the Product team would provide and analyze a reasonable number to ensure a constant flow of work, and ask the teams simply to deliver as much as they could.

The teams agreed to try this new approach, with very positive results. The teams were much more relaxed, energy levels improved, and planning became much shorter. However, the teams were still delivering as much working, tested software as possible each sprint, while maintaining a sustainable pace and avoiding technical debt.

> **REDUCE**
>
> *We started this book with this quote:*
>
> *"Perfection is achieved not when there is nothing to add, but when there is nothing to take away."*
> *~ Antoine de Saint-Exupery*
>
> *FiftyOne's major process improvements come from installing a process and then paring away the elements that don't work in their context.*

In fact, quantitative results also started showing improvements in team delivery, without any drop in product quality. This improved delivery was supported greatly by the fact that the Engineering teams were generally highly motivated and working on stories with a clear business purpose, e.g. increasing the rate at which potential customers followed through by purchasing the product.

This was a particularly exciting point in the team's evolution, since it was the first evidence of kanban-style thinking—pull rather than push—starting to manifest in this group.

DO WE NEED A SPRINT REVIEW?

Early on, the team agreed that the Product team should demo and accept stories throughout the sprint as each story was completed. This was part of the storyboard process flow.

While this introduced hand-offs within the sprint and challenged their ability to commit as a team, the process worked relatively smoothly. A particular challenge around this arose over weekends when there were long windows where the US-based Product team wasn't available while the Israeli team continued to work on Sundays. When the team in Israel finished stories on Sunday they often waited until the end of Monday to get feedback from the Product team. With code going into freeze on Wednesdays, there was a repeated push to accommodate demo feedback from the Product team on Tuesdays. This created an frantic spike in activity on Tuesdays, with substantial idle wait times on the preceding days.

One of the countermeasures the team adopted was to use the Local Product Owner for demos on the Sunday-Monday before sprint-end and to ensure that the east coast Product Manager handled demos first thing on Monday morning. This left some time on Mondays for the Israel-based teams to deal with feedback.

Interestingly, the team then started asking whether there was still a need for a sprint review if stories were being reviewed and accepted during the sprint. A decision was made to keep the sprint review as an opportunity for the whole

> ## NO, ACTUALLY THIS WORKS
>
> *This section is important because we are seeing something rarely reported: the decision not to change. The FiftyOne team had real questions about the efficacy of the Sprint Review. They discussed and ran experiments, finally ending up keeping them with only slight augmentation.*

team to get together to see the full picture of what was delivered and to celebrate it. Over time, the sprint reviews did become shorter, but they continue to be held and add value to the team as a whole.

EVOLVING FURTHER TO SCRUMBAN

Approximately three to four months into its agile transition, the team reflected on what they had achieved, and where they wanted to go next. It was clear that Agile/Scrum was a significant improvement on the way they used to do things. The team identified its fast cadence, the renewed energies and the level of team empowerment as significant benefits.

Still, there remained strong sense that the team could continue to improve, especially around how they dealt with sprints. Although the sprint commitment had already become a more fluid measurement, the need to "clean the board" after every sprint caused flow problems as it emphasized and exacerbated testing bottlenecks while creating empty pockets of idle time.

The AgileSparks coaches thought the time may be ripe for a more flow-oriented approach that drew inspiration from Kanban. This time, with the teams already comfortably in place, it seemed like a more feasible option, and the teams adapted to the change almost seamlessly.

After a day-long workshop to examine the differences between Scrum and Kanban, the teams simply started to work using Kanban. As they were already familiar with Agile, and in fact were already using some aspects of pull, the workshop served primarily to learn more about effectively limiting Work-in-Progress (WIP), how to choose WIP limits, how to deal with defects, and other specific scenarios the team were unsure of in the context of Kanban.

> ## THE PRESSURE OF VISUALIZATION
>
> *Work that is visualized but not completed applies psychological pressure. The team, still thinking in sprints, wanted to "clear the board," even if they didn't promise to. Likewise, bottlenecks or other problems visualized on the board compel us to find a solution.*
>
> *The solution: reinterpret the board as a true flow system and not the visualization of an iterative system.*

BEYOND AGILE

TESTING THE AGILE WAY

The team spent considerable time deciding how to effectively do software testing in an agile environment, and how to realistically model this work on the kanban board. It is also the single biggest area that underwent significant evolution over time.

Initially, stories were handed off to testing after the development was done. Not surprisingly, this proved hard to do in short sprints. At this stage Testing was a separate lane on the team board. However, some testing was often already being done on the story while it was in the Development phase. This was a challenge for the kanban board to present, until the team decided to add tasks under each story.

The next change came when the team realized that there was a lot of collaboration between developers and testers during the supposed **Development** phase, and that this work was in fact testing.

> ## MORE THAN ONE WAY
>
> *In Scrumban, Corey Ladas describes this type of visualization. Previously, the team considered Test as the activity of testers. Now, they see that there are different types of testing that happen at different times in the development process. Test and Adv Testing are now solely elements of work flow and do not relate directly to the job descriptions of those doing the work.*

The team decided to model this behavior by changing **Development** to **Dev&Test**, with a separate lane for **Adv Testing** that would sometimes remain after the initial testing. Although developers initially sometimes had to help out with **Adv Testing,** as the team has become more efficient—in large part due to improved automation testing—**Adv Testing** has become less of a bottleneck. The bulk of the functional testing is now completed during the **Dev&Test** phase, leaving **Adv Testing** for exploratory, usability, and user acceptance testing.

DRIVING FROM ACCEPTANCE TESTS

Another testing challenge for this team was how to align the developers and testers more closely, specifically regarding what to develop and what to test, and how to reduce testing bottleneck by having developers collaborate more deeply in the testing effort. The team experimented with ATDD (Acceptance Test Driven Development), and found that it certainly improved things. Testers could now guide developers in what to test, what to automate, and there is generally a stronger common understanding of the story and how it should work.

Getting to this point did not happen overnight, however. Since testers were required to define acceptance tests upfront using this technique, they now became a bottleneck before development had even started. This happened mainly because of two reasons:

⇨ Testers still had testing work to do that the developers were not really helping with, They couldn't free up time to go and work in front of the developers. Over time, offloading some of the automation work to developers solved this issue.

⇨ Testers were new to acceptance tests and they took long to define them. They were used to defining complete test cases and weren't really sure how comprehensive the acceptance tests should be.

These two root causes manifested in one of two ways— either slack time where developers didn't have stories they could start working on or developers pulling stories that did not have acceptance tests.

The workload was smoothed out by changing to a more lightweight definition of acceptance tests up front, and elaborating on them later in the **Dev&Test** phase. The coaches also introduced some of Janet Gregory's tips and tricks from her Agile Testing[1] Workshop. One that worked especially well was the approach of writing a few key acceptance tests on a note during the story elaboration meeting, and sharing these notes with the developers right after the meeting so that they would at least have an initial glimpse at the test plan.

HOW MUCH QUALITY IS ENOUGH?

A general concern often expressed about testing in Agile, Scrum and especially Kanban, is that testing is something you can never have enough of. Testers are often perfectionists and are held accountable for minimizing the amount of escaping defects and sometimes also for the number of defects found. In classic phase-driven approaches, and to some extent also in timebox-driven approaches like Scrum, there is a limit to how much time

---

[1]   http://www.janetgregory.ca/

there is for testing. Usually, there is not even enough time for testing, and certainly the dynamics force some risk-taking on the part of the testing effort. Also, in classic approaches testing by implication has to be more risk-averse since the product quality handed off to them is often lower since developers rely on the testers to find the issues.

In Kanban, since teams are working in pull mode, without a push-driven deadline for each phase of the work and usually without a committed date for the stories to be completed, there is little to box the testing effort, at least in the usual way. Testing can start taking up more time than is warranted by the quality being built into the software throughout the development process.

This was evident in the FiftyOne team, specifically in the time it took testers to write acceptance tests and the time used for Adv Testing. Guided by the AgileSparks coaches, the team employed a number of techniques to counteract this behavior, proactively led by a very enthusiastic and change-tolerant QA Manager.

These techniques include the following:

⇨ WIP limits provide some positive pressure to deliver and prevent testing from being a bottleneck. At a minimum, once a bottleneck is identified, the WIP provides an opportunity to stop the line and discuss what to do at team-level. Problems cannot manifest for long without surfacing to the conscience of the team.

⇨ Scrumban sprints or cadences provide another form of positive pressure to deliver. While the commitment is less specific, the fact that there is a delivery date and you want your stories to be part of this delivery energizes and keeps teams focused.

⇨ The vision and sense of purpose provided by the Product Owner for features that the team is working on, help to raise the sense of urgency.

⇨ Real external commitments, like delivering features for a specific client project, make for much better motivation than abstract, internal virtual commitments.

⇨ Measuring velocity and cycle time and presenting it to the team, and agreeing to try and stabilize and improve it, provides another type of motivation. The message here is that we are trying to become more fit, not trying to "make" the sprint.

⇨ Measuring escaping defects also keeps test scope in check and shows that, despite accelerating velocity, the team is still providing great quality. If the number of escaping defects increases, then it's time to slow down again.

From a coaching perspective, creating motivation in continuous flow-driven product development is particularly interesting. Based on the empiric evidence from a number of cases, it appears that a mix of the above points works best, depending on the nature of the product and the team. However, in most cases, a regular, established cadence is usually an important cornerstone of an effective product development flow system.

WHO PULLS WHOM?

In Lean, pull is a dynamic concept. Value is pulled through a system. Developers, testers, and managers are all part of that system. No matter what you are creating, it needs to have demonstrable customer value.

The current growing kanban rhetoric is that developers pull the work they want when they want. This is true to the extent that the developer is locally optimizing their time and effort to create customer value.

So, while the developer should feel better about being in more control of the completion of their immediate work, it is important to note that the customer is pulling the developer.

Another crucial point is having a very clear picture of what it means to be done with each phase of the work—the "Definition of Done." Once the FiftyOne team visually captured their Definition of Done for each phase, it also helped to balance the line. In addition, a cap was put on the amount of time to spend on ATDD (exploratory testing) per story as well as other similar open-ended activities.

More importantly, however, as Yuval relates:

"The team was becoming more and more adept at identifying issues, discussing them, and coming up with solutions. This increased the courage of the team and its management to keep on experimenting and improving."

PERFORMANCE INDICATORS

Operational Review

Somewhere along the move to Scrumban, the team started to run operational reviews that provide data-driven discussions beyond the sprint retrospectives. Now that they have the overall process more or less under control, they are focusing more and more on reducing variability and improving predictability.

This section highlights some of the empirical results seen in this team during their transition from Scrum to continuous delivery. These reviews are based on data from the electronic board in AgileZen as well as Excel extracts of the board data using the AgileZen API.

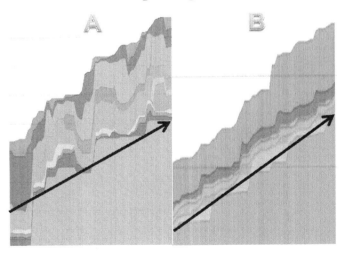

Cumulative Flow 2 months (A) and 12 months (B) into the Agile journey

Both experienced and new Kanban practitioners easily point to B as being the better behaving system. The amount of WIP in each colored phase is clearly lower in

B, leading to a reduction in cycle time and more work delivered over time. In addition, B is much more predictable and "nice-looking"—a typical observation made by people seeing Continuous Flow Diagrams (CFDs) for the first time.

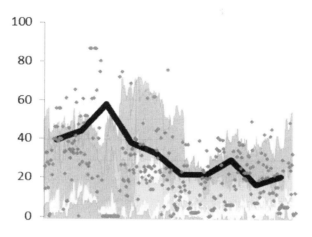

Queues, WIP and Cycle Time throughout the agile journey

Note the expected correlation between a reduction of WIP and an improvement in the average cycle time, as well as cycle time becoming more predictable as seen below in Figure 5. Other elements that contributed to reduction of cycle time were the use of ATDD leading to stories passing through **Dev&Test** more efficiently, as well as bringing the story size under control.

While there are still ups and downs, some of them related to seasonality (e.g. a holiday deployment freeze period), the overall trend is clear.

ONGOING CHALLENGES

Scaling Scrumban to Multiple Teams—How to Pull from the Product Backlog

Working with two teams on the same product presented some challenges when the team considered pull-based approaches. Since the product backlog is shared between teams, the question of how stories should be pulled into teams came up.

The initial approach was for the Local Product Owner (LPO) to assign a story to a specific team during analysis. Since the LPO has knowledge of the capabilities of the teams and their approximate current load, he was able to make reasonably valid assignments. In addition, this saved on the synchronization costs between the teams, and provided some global optimization, e.g. ensuring a team didn't take a story when the other team would be better at it or would be able to pull it very soon.

This is of course somewhat of a push mechanism, and certainly not very self-organized. At some point the group experimented with the teams simply pulling from the product backlog without initial assignment by the LPO. This did

> ### WELL, MAYBE NOT
>
> *What may actually be happening here is the LPO is serving in their role as the voice of the customer. There is customer value that is not being pulled by the locally-optimizing (self-organizing) team. Therefore, the LPO is making sure that the overlooked customer value is worked on.*
>
> *This is a pull system.*

not work very well. The teams didn't feel comfortable with this method, and preferred to be fed stories, at least at this point in time.

With the number of teams now growing from two to four due to growth of the overall group size, it's becoming increasingly harder to make wise central up-front decisions regarding assignment. The team has therefore again started experimenting with self-assignment, but whether this is the most effective solution still remains to be seen.

Reducing Variability and Increasing Predictability

With the production line now more or less balanced, the team's concerns are continuing to shift to how they can improve their throughput by improving effectiveness and eliminating unhealthy variability. Armed with the data from the statistical process control charts, the teams have now also started using Root Cause Analysis (RCA) on common causes of variability.

THE ROAD TO SUCCESS

This is a classic example of an organization making the transition to Scrum, and then evolving to Scrumban to try and run a leaner Scrum process. The team exhibited some aspects of lean thinking all along, making this a very natural transition.

The combination of flow-driven Kanban, together with the initial structure of Scrum, proved very successful for this team. A significant driver behind this success was the fact that the managers of the group were very engaged in continuous improvement, working as a team to identify areas that could be optimized.

Inside the team, the key to achieving healthy flow was changing the traditional testing mindset. Testers are now no longer responsible for all the testing work. Testers may set the testing strategy and approach, but the team as a whole takes ownership of that approach. This mindset shift made it possible to implement practices like ATDD and shared ownership of test automation.

To sum up, here is what Ben Peer had to say about his organization's transformation:

Our engineering organization has transitioned from quarterly releases into two week releases using Scrum and Kanban. We've switched from complex, obscure, inefficient and difficult Gantts into a highly visual kanban board in which you can understand in seconds your project status and, even more importantly, literally see our development process challenges. This builds a continuous improvement culture.

The transition, or rather journey, from Waterfall to Agile has helped to surface all of our development deficiencies and improvement opportunities, and with courage we handled those and we still continue to do so after five months (ten sprints).

Through the transition, from Sprint #1 until the present date, we've deployed on our production site new user stories with true business value to a very complex platform and also scaled up the R&D team significantly. In addition to the obvious benefits of the R&D improvements, our business can react much faster than before to market needs and to internal organization needs as our business continues to grow.

The executive team led by the CEO is very pleased with the results and sees the transition as successful and appreciates the added value we now bring to the company.

~ Ben Peer

CODA
MAKING BEYOND AGILE

THE MAKING OF BEYOND AGILE

(or Herding Picasso's Cubist Cats)

VITAL STATISTICS

Company: Modus Cooperandi
Location: Seattle, USA
Industry and Domain: Publishing, Consultancy
Dates: August 2010 – February 2013
Team Size: Core team of three to five people at various times
Distributed: Yes
Level of Distribution: *Constantly randomly distributed.* The core team is based in Seattle, with Maritza in South Africa. However, none of the team members have in fact ever met Maritza (except Maritza, of course), apart

from Skype, Twitter and email conversations. In addition, Joanne lived in Belgium for part of the writing of the book and Jim is more likely to be found in an airport than at home.

BACKGROUND

As the content of this book hopefully attests, our idea was to collect and collate case studies on the application of continuous improvement in teams. We set out to cover a range of industries and geographies to illustrate the principles that Jim writes about in the Introduction. Making this happen required a range of activities, from canvassing and approaching potential contributors for written submissions, to interviewing and writing up contributions on behalf of contributors.

All of this had to be done while juggling a number of time zones as well as work and travel schedules, as none of the authors could commit to working on the book full-time, and the contributors from the various companies also had their own projects, deadlines, and travels.

It is no wonder that our process saw significant evolution over the course of two years. Much of this evolution was the result of the highly collaborative authoring approach.

EVOLUTION OF DESIGN

Story Format and Quantity

The single biggest evolution has been the very nature of the book itself. We did not start out with a fixed format in mind for the book. Jim basically said he wanted to do a follow-up on the Scrumban book, and that the follow-up would be a collection of real-world cases of applying the principles espoused by Corey Ladas.

This loose definition (*read: ill-defined requirement*) led to some initial thrashing around the way stories should be written and made it hard to establish consistency of tone and content between the early contributions. For a time, I was concerned the stories were not scientific enough, and that would invalidate the book. However, when Jim made it clear his vision was in fact to tell stories about continuous improvement, highlighting the human element underneath the science and the facts, the format and tone of the stories started to settle.

Book Structure

At the outset, we created a basic chapter layout, with basic guidelines for the scope of information he wanted each story to include. Armed with this layout, we canvassed our respective contacts and requested potential authors to write according to the guidelines. In quite a few cases, the people we approached were too busy to write up their story. In these cases, we gave them the option of being interviewed via telephone, after which we wrote the actual story.

Through this approach, we were lucky to find as many as 19 volunteers quite quickly. However, as we started finalizing the stories and thematic possibilities started emerging, some stories were left out of the final book, as they either duplicated a point already made or did not fit the narrative style that had by then emerged.

The final ordering of stories in the book was also open-ended for quite some time. In fact, only when about 80% of the final shortlist of stories was complete, did the eventual three-part structure suggest itself. We were particularly excited when this happened, as it represented that moment when we could really "see" the book for the first time.

Evolution of Cadence

This aspect of our work process has certainly been the most erratic. At the outset, we had to decide how often we would get together and how long we would work on this book. Our initial plans were roughly "finish the book within nine months and have a Skype call to check in on progress every two weeks."

These plans, like so many plans of so many teams before us, were not rooted in the reality of our individual work and life commitments and were very soon exposed to in fact be complete wishful thinking. We diligently started with a call every second week, but they didn't hold for long because of the widely conflicting travel schedules and time zone challenges between the three core participants at the time. And we realized that, due to our primary commitments, we couldn't really rely on making steady progress between calls either.

About a year into the project, shortly after Joanne joined us, we acknowledged and addressed this explicitly, something that was long-overdue on the project. Instead of continuing to feel guilty about what *we could not do*, we agreed to *work when we can, adapting to each other's schedules and availability.* We started working in bursts. There were slow periods during which each team member had their own full-time projects and work to attend to, followed by windows of opportunity where book work continued at a faster rate.

At about this time, we re-instituted our team calls again, now weekly. We had more success with them this time around, particularly because we had by then identified that the calls were only possible when there was a quorum present in Seattle to anchor it. If we were all travelling, particularly abroad, we simply skipped that week's check-in and picked up again a week later.

The real magic, however, came when we turned these weekly calls into actual Pomodoros, or working sessions. Instead of just having an update call, we would actually work together remotely for an hour (or two) depending on how much time each could contribute that day. Working like this, with Skype turned on for any questions that may come up, we established a form of virtual "collocation". This provided the long-absent benefits of collegial camaraderie and the joy of celebrating progress together as it happened.

Finally, as the book was nearing completion, we added a second optional team call to keep the momentum up and to ensure that anybody who missed the one call could still get their questions answered in the other one.

Evolution of Visual Controls

As you'd expect from a team of kanban practitioners, we set up a cloud-based kanban that tracked our work over the lifetime of the project. This kanban worked well—naturally evolving as we learnt about our work process—and lasted throughout the project.

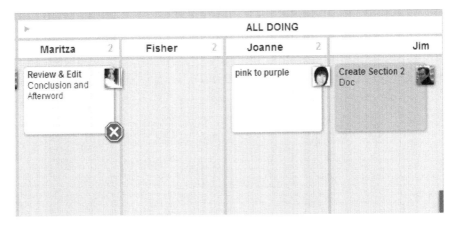

The extended timeframe and nature of the project also led to another set of visual controls that was especially useful as a way of communicating project changes and status. Early on, we decided to house the growing manuscript in Google Docs (now Drive). This gave our writing team, as well as all the contributors, real-time access to the material and helped us to keep a folder-based visual history of the various rounds of editing on each story.

TALES OF CONTINUOUS IMPROVEMENT

Another advantage of Google Docs turned out to be that it alerted us automatically whenever somebody had been working on the project. There were three major types of changes to the documents – new writing, edits, and comments – all of which cause documents to rise to the top when you use the "Recent Changes" view.

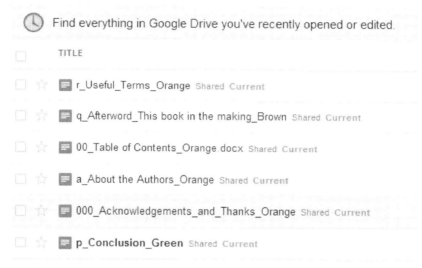

About halfway through the project, when the structure and ordering of stories had started to settle, we created a *Table of Contents* to reflect the agreed ordering. Within a few weeks, this turned into our master visual control when we started using colors with a detailed legend to track the progress of individual stories and book components through our writing workflow.

While our kanban showed us *who* was doing *what*, this view showed us *overall project progress and status* in one easily interpreted—and very meaningful—view.

Evolution of Commentary Style

As we team collected stories, we could see that each story did a good job of describing the "case study" of its own narrative and added to an overall narrative. We thought initially we would relate each story back to the original principles described in the introduction. However, what evolved was much different. The emerging narrative of the book didn't require such a self-righteous approach.

The meta-narrative of continuous improvement was carried by the strength of the case studies. We opted instead to use callout boxes to highlight the fascinating things that were happening in each story. Rather than providing commentary that overly editorialized, we let the case studies speak for themselves.

This was not an easy transition. At any point in time, you could find healthy debate going on right in the documents. As our team was writing and editing the stories, we were actively discussing what the stories actually meant. Sometimes those discussions were frank and apparently critical of the decisions being made in the stories themselves.

As these conversations were happening, not only was our understanding of the individual stories evolving, but so was our individual appreciation of the difficulties of continuous improvement in the face of very real challenges.

The Big Bad: Exceeding WIP

We made an obvious mistake in the early phases of the project. In our enthusiasm to get started, we conducted a lot of interviews and canvassed for a lot of submissions in a short time without considering our capacity to process these contributions and interviews.

The result was an extremely long cycle time on the earlier contributions. Contributors had to deal patiently with long periods of silence from us, as we were steadily making our way through the backlog of contributions. Even more disturbingly, by the time we wrote up some of the interviews, it was difficult to make sense of some of the audio recordings and rapid fire notes that were taken during interviews. This affected the quality of some of the write-ups, and required additional e-mails, Skype chats or interviews to verify the content.

Altogether now: *Can everybody say "Rework due to low quality resulting from Exceeding Work In Progress and Cost of Delay"?*

In hindsight: We should have done fewer submissions at a time (perhaps even one?) This project was an ideal candidate for single piece workflow with early feedback and incremental delivery of the published result à la Lean publishing.

Towards the end of the project, this specific mistake caught up with us again in another guise. Those stories that had required most rework were the ones lagging behind in making it through specific checkpoints and gates. And, woe upon woe, we had one of these stories in each Part of the book! Each Part is a cohesive whole for us, which meant that one story in each Part was holding up the entire Part.

Altogether now: *Can everybody say: "Launch delays resulting from failure to batch work sensibly"?*

The most painful consequence of this particular mistake in our work process was the disappointment it caused for some or our contributors. Not only did we create expectations around time to publish that we could not meet, but we eventually found that we had to drop a small number of stories from the book because they were covering aspects already covered by another story, and because we wanted to finalize and ship the book.

The Powerful Good: Trust

When you set aside all the pragmatics of the writing approach, process tools and visual indicators, you might begin to marvel at the fact you are reading this book today at all. What was the secret sauce that kept it all together in the end? One word: Trust.

That trust was born out of working and solving problems together, respecting our individual perspectives and expertise, and expecting professionalism and integrity from one another as a matter of course. Even when deadlines were slipping, and during times when we didn't communicate as effectively as we ideally should've, I could always rely on the fact that somebody on the other side of the ocean would eventually get back to me, or move a task forward, whether that somebody was Jim, Joanne or (for quite some time) our very cool, calm and collected production assistant, Fisher S. Qua.

IN RETROSPECT

Being project manager, Scrum Master and principal author was far from ideal. I would often put my head down and write, leaving some project management tasks undone, and vice versa. This often left me feeling that I was letting myself, the team and our contributors down. But as I came to accept our team for what it was—a loose collective of people, trying to produce a book together in the precious little spare time they had—I came to accept the inevitability of our stuttering rhythm.

Should we then ever have attempted to write this book, you might ask? Heaven knows, I have often asked myself that question. We were all busy people already, with busy working lives, families, and sometimes other parallel projects to take care of. Why then tackle this project which was clearly a significant challenge to each individual's WIP limit?

Because these stories had to be told. They're real stories about real teams and real people, all trying to deliver the best work they can by taking responsibility for the way they work, often flying in the face of well-established and enshrined processes in their organizations. They're brave stories. And if even one story in this book inspires another team in another organization somewhere in the world to be brave, then the many long nights and weekends have been a small price to pay.

That said—knowing what I know now—I would never recommend this approach to anybody, nor would I ever do it again. At least, not with the same mistakes! And that, ultimately, is what continuous improvement is about.

Thank you for witnessing our story.

Maritza van den Heuvel
Cape Town, South Africa
February 2013

AFTERWORD

▶ **If you don't make mistakes, you're not reaching far enough.** ~ *David Packard*

In the ten stories of evolving teams in this book, you have seen a spectrum of change behavior play out in real working environments. Some companies made drastic changes to their organization that helped them to be wildly successful. Others attempted similar changes, but with little impact beyond their own teams. Some even had abysmal results.

Your success in building and maintaining happy, productive teams depends on not only your application of the principles illustrated in the book, but also on the viability of your environment and external constraints. The principles provide a specific frame for actions in the context of your environment.

It is our hope to arm you not with alleged "facts," but with an appreciation for some of the more collaborative, value-driven options you have so that you and your co-workers can apply them thoughtfully to your specific challenges. Achieving a sustainable workflow for your team, one that delivers real customer value without destroying the people doing the work, is something one can only learn by doing. The stories in this book have been provided by individuals and teams who wished to share both the pain and the joy of their experiences to encourage you to brave the journey through continuous improvement. Stories can only influence the decisions you make for yourself and your team; they cannot make decisions for you.

At the core of Agile, these principles all ask that you examine the way you work critically. Hold the status quo up to inspection and adapt where necessary. *What is your value stream? How much Work-in-Progress is too much? What does your work really look like? What are your real constraints? How can you help work smoothly through your team? Most importantly, how can you bring about a culture of continuous improvement to enable real systemic change?*

THE LESSONS OF BEYOND AGILE

Attachmate and **Rally** have shown how the use of a visual tool such as a kanban board can make work visible and help you to find efficiencies. Similarly, Fundamo discovered that having less forces you to focus your energy and resources to create a process that is specific to your team, instead of mechanically following a prescribed process. And **Getty Images** is a good example of successful process evolution in a large organization—this isn't just for small companies.

Both **Socialtext** and **WIKISPEED** illustrate that good process is limited without transparent collaboration. At Socialtext we saw how embracing radical transparency turned a toxic culture into a highly collaborative, high-performing one, while WIKISPEED has used sound design principles to enable distributed, self-organizing teams to work collaboratively, yet independently. For **Innvo**, improving work didn't just mean improving their own process, but also extending their collaboration across team boundaries, thereby improving the end-to-end flow of work in the organization.

BrainStore is a reminder that experiments in process change require involvement of those experiencing the change for change to be sustainable. **CCRTV**, on the other hand, is an equally strong example of the outcome of process change as a series of carefully monitored experiments, each designed to address a real business need. **FiftyOne** shows us a logical, methodologically sound, data-driven process improvement effort that was not only successful, but still managed to balance commercial business concerns with Agile and Lean principles.

And finally, our own story is a reality check, to warn you that, even when you know the theory and have applied it many times before successfully, you don't always get it right. You still make mistakes. Get used to it. For it's from the mistakes that we learn how to do it better.

SHAPING THE FUTURE OF YOUR TEAM

We often think of the future as an endless journey down an infinitely long road and feel overwhelmed because we cannot see the end of that road. To become a healthy, collaborative and productive team or organization, you

BEYOND AGILE

do not need to know the exact outcome right now. You just have to take those first small steps on the path to improvement. You can start today by:

1. Visualizing all your work

2. Limiting Work-in-Progress

3. Identifying blockages that interrupt the flow of work

4. Eliminating blockages by adapting as needed

5. Addressing any factors that prevent you from improving

By applying these steps repeatedly and thoughtfully, you will continue discovering your own emergent process.

Happy improving!

Joanne Ho
Seattle, Washington, USA
February, 2013

ABOUT THE AUTHORS

MARITZA

Maritza van den Heuvel spent six years doing research in computational linguistics after completing a Postgraduate degree in Linguistics. She eventually left academia for the software industry where she cut her teeth on Agile and Scrum as a Scrum Master and Product Owner, helping teams to evolve from waterfall to Scrum. Along the way, her unquenchable thirst for knowledge led her to Kanban and Lean systems thinking. Since then, she has become a passionate proponent of the power of constraints and visual controls to transform the world of work in the 21st century. She is currently with Pearson Southern Africa, where she's applying her background to leading innovation in technology-enabled education.

At heart, Maritza is a writer. She is the author of the Becoming an Agile Family blog where she writes about the ways her family uses Personal Kanban to navigate work and life. To learn more about Maritza and her passion for continuous improvement, go to www.scrumfamily.wordpress.com or find her on Twitter (@maritzavdh).

JIM

Jim Benson's background in psychology, urban planning, and software development has seen him build light rail systems and neighborhoods, enterprise software and web sites and, most recently, help create better working environments for teams of all sizes as the CEO of Modus Cooperandi. The common thread throughout his history has been the systems, collaboration, and methods of problem solving.

With Modus, Jim has worked with corporate, government, and not-for-profit organizations of all sizes. He helps clients create sustainable collaborative / Lean management systems. He and his company combine Lean principles from manufacturing, Agile methodologies from software design, and the recent revelations in cognitive psychology as process and tool infrastructure.

Jim is the creator of Personal Kanban, a system for visualizing and controlling knowledge work, and a pioneer in the field of Lean Management for knowledge workers. His book with Tonianne DeMaria Barry, Personal Kanban, is a global bestseller and 2013 winner of the Shingo Prize for Operational Excellence. He is also a fellow in the Lean Systems Society and a 2012 winner of the Brickell Key Award for Excellence in Lean Thinking.

He loves to eat and hates PowerPoint.

He is @ourfounder on Twitter.

JOANNE

Joanne Ho is the founder of PowerHouse360, a real estate company committed to building and creating living environments with positive internal and external impacts on our society and environment – physically, mentally, emotionally, and spiritually. During her doctoral studies, Joanne applied Agile methodologies to her PhD research. As an environmental researcher, she adopted tools from Scrum and Kanban to manage environmental research projects conducted by her interdisciplinary team. She used Agile methods to organize innovative processes to plan and drive research, a process of discovery involving a road map to the unknown.

Joanne is currently writing an Agile project management guidebook for graduate students. Joanne holds a PhD in Forest Resources (University of Washington) and MA in International Economics (University of Sussex). To learn more about Joanne and her company, go to www.power-house360.com

MODUS COOPERANDI PRESS

GROUNDBREAKING WORKS IN CONTINUOUS IMPROVEMENT

SCRUMBAN

By Corey Ladas

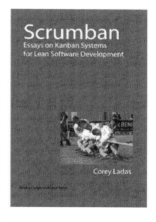

If you enjoyed this book, the foundations of it rest firmly in Corey Ladas' groundbreaking book "Scrumban." Scrumban captured the imagination of the software development world and led teams to not only begin continuous improvement efforts, but do so with a new and exciting set of tools. Scrum and Agile methodologies have helped software development teams organize and become more efficient. Lean methods like Kanban can extend these benefits. Kanban also provides a powerful mechanism to identify process improvement opportunities. This book covers some of the metrics and day-to-day management techniques that make continuous improvement an achievable outcome in the real world. ScrumBan the book provides a series of essays that give practitioners the background needed to create more robust practices combining the best of Agile and Lean.

PERSONAL KANBAN

By Jim Benson and Tonianne DeMaria Barry

Winner of the 2013 Shingo Prize.

Machines need to be productive. People need to be effective. Productivity books focus on doing more, Jim and Tonianne want you to focus on doing better. Personal Kanban is about choosing the right work at the right time; recognizing why we do the things we do; understanding the impact of our actions; creating value – not just product. For ourselves, our families, our friends, our co-workers. For our legacy. Personal Kanban takes the same Lean principles from manufacturing that led the Japanese auto industry to become a global leader in quality, and applies them to individual and team work. Personal Kanban asks only that we visualize our work and limit our work-in-progress. Visualizing work allows us to transform our conceptual and threatening workload into an actionable, context-sensitive flow. Limiting our work-in-progress helps us complete what we start and understand the value of our choices. Combined, these two simple acts encourage us to improve the way we work and the way we make choices to balance our personal, professional, and social lives. Neither a prescription nor a plan, Personal Kanban provides a light, actionable, achievable framework for understanding our work and its context. This book describes why students, parents, business leaders, major corporations, and world governments all see immediate results with Personal Kanban.

WHY PLANS FAIL

By Jim Benson

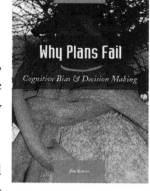

Business runs on decisions. Recently, we've discovered that people aren't the great decision makers we thought they were.

Business relies on estimates, plans, and projections – and we all know how accurate they tend to be. Careers are made and careers are broken based on accurate estimation and planning.

But what if the successes and failures of these projects were not based on the prowess of those making the plans? What if success or failure were more often the result of a more complex set of events?

Why Plans Fail directly addresses our ability of to plan, to forecast, and to make decisions.

Written by Jim Benson, an urban planner, software developer, and business owner who has planned and built everything from small software projects, to houses, to urban freeway systems – Why Plans Fail is told by someone with much skin in the estimation and planning game.

This short work is the first in the Modus Cooperandi MemeMachine series, which looks specifically at underlying issues that directly impact the success of teams, companies, and individuals. The MemeMachine series is meant to start conversations and advance discussion.

WHITE PAPER 1: KANBAN: DIVERSITY AND OPTIMIZATION OF KNOWLEDGE WORKING TEAMS

By Jim Benson

KINDLE ONLY

Late in 2012, we conducted a Board Walk (a site visit where we meet with teams using Kanban or Personal Kanban and help them optimize the board and the team itself) at a client in the United States. There were 15 individual teams, each of which had its own individually designed boards. Each board had a unique value stream, work item types, policies, and methods for judging completeness and quality.

Both management and the teams were frustrated because they hadn't yet found a board design that worked for the entire company. They were looking for standardization.

However, each of these boards were, in some way, optimized for each individual team. Each team had its own context and these boards related specifically to that context. Each team was also actively improving their boards on a regular basis – meaning that optimization was continuing.

This white paper contrasts many of these boards, showing the differences in design of each board and the ramifications of those variations.

WHITE PAPER 2: THE CLIENT MANAGEMENT A3

By Jim Benson

KINDLE ONLY

We examine a mashup between the Lean A3 decision making and experimentation tool and the Persona tool from software development. The blend of these two techniques provides insights both into controlled business process experimentation and the recognition of the impacts of individuals in our processes.

USEFUL TERMS

DE-JARGONATOR

The world is filled with jargon. In this book we tried to avoid it and found that simply was impossible. This type of work has its own language, as does project management. Therefore, we have provided definitions for some of the most notable Agile and Lean software development terms you will come across in our book. This is by no means an exhaustive list of all terms that are (sometimes in passing) referred to in this book, but we trust it serves as a starting point for further exploration. KEEP READING!

Agile (Software Development) A methodology for the creative process that anticipates the need for flexibility and applies a level of pragmatism into the delivery of the finished product. The goal is to build upon small client-approved parts as the project progresses, as opposed to delivering one large application at the end of the project. Increasingly, Agile is used as a blanket term outside of software development to describe processes that are flexible and iterative.

Automated Unit Tests Automating a manual process already in place to control specific, granular and discrete tests that test individual code unites in isolation to the rest of the software.

Backlog A term that originated from the Agile and Scrum concept of "work to be done." It is a list of tasks, features, and work that needs to be completed. Work-in-Progress is pulled from this prioritized list.

(Backlog) Grooming In Agile software development methods, a practice where business people and technical teams discuss the content of work to be done to inform story point estimation and iteration planning.

Black-box Testing Tests the end-user functionality of an application as opposed to its internal structures or workings.

Bot An automated software program that can execute certain commands when it receives a specific input. This is most common in internet chatrooms or help sites and in search engine cataloging & indexing.

Bottleneck A term common in Lean and Kanban software development that refers to a resource constraint (people or process) that causes workflow and throughput to be restricted.

Burndown A chart used by Agile teams that reflects the amount of work left to do (or tasks to complete) relative to the time left to complete it.

Cadence In Agile and Lean methodologies, cadence refers to the regular work rhythm (or heartbeat) that a team develops over time as it works together. In Scrum, the cadence is somewhat artificially represented by the defined Sprint duration. In Kanban, the cadence emerges over time based on the work delivered by the team.

Class of Service A functional designation for a piece of work based on its importance or project impact. Classes of service can vary from project to project. Common classifications might include: Planned Work, Emergency, and Induced Work.

Continuous Integration (CI) A software engineering practice where isolated changes are added to and tested in context of a larger system on an ongoing basis as they are developed. It aims to improve the overall quality of the system and to reduce the risks associated with integrated a large number of changes simultaneously in the system.

Conversion Rate Refers to the ratio of visitors who convert casual content views or website visits into desired actions based on subtle or direct requests from marketers, advertisers, and content creators (usually used in internet marketing).

Cross Functional Teams Teams that include many different skill sets, as opposed to a siloed team which would have only one skill set (e.g. a testing team).

Cumulative Flow Diagram (CFD) A cumulative flow diagram is tool used in queuing theory. It is an area graph that depicts the quantity of work in a given state, showing arrivals, time in queue, quantity in queue, and departure.

Cycle Time The period required to complete one cycle of an operation; or to complete a function, job, or task from start to finish. When used in lean and/or kanban software development environments, this refers to the mean or average time for a work item to pass through the workstream.

Definition of Done In Agile development, an agreement within a team that explicitly defines what steps need to be covered for a piece of work to be considered "Done". Typical examples of such steps are Design, Coding, Peer Review, Testing, Documentation and PO Review.

Developer A person concerned with the technical aspects of the software development process. Their work includes researching, designing, developing, and testing software. Gathers requirements, designs and implements applications, researches technologies, etc.

Emergent Design An approach to designing software that applies minimal design initially, and applies incremental design techniques to allow the design of the system to evolve as the software requires.

Engineer Often used interchangeably with "developer". In the strict sense, however, engineers design and implement components and frameworks for Developers and Programmers to use.

Extreme Programming (XP) A software development methodology which is intended to improve software quality and responsiveness to changing customer requirements. As a type of Agile software development, it advocates frequent "releases" in short development cycles (timeboxing), which is intended to improve productivity and introduce checkpoints where new customer requirements can be adopted.

Features A distinguishing characteristic of a software item (e.g., performance, portability, or functionality)

(Feature) Requirements A way to capture functional requirements as use cases or some similar mechanism (e.g. user stories, PRD & Specs for example). These are compiled into documents that guide the development of the product and contains elements such as:

⇨ Feature List –This can be on a sheet of notebook paper.

⇨ Vision Document

⇨ Use Case Outlines

⇨ Use Case Details

⇨ Use Case Diagrams

⇨ Supplemental (Non-Functional) Requirements

Fibonacci Number In mathematics, the Fibonacci numbers or Fibonacci series or Fibonacci sequence are the numbers in the following integer sequence 1, 1, 2, 3, 5, 8, 13, 21, 34, 55, 89, 144

J-Curve Refers to a variety of unrelated J-shaped statistical diagrams where a curve initially falls, but then demonstrates a rising trend.

Lead Time The latency (delay) between the initiation and execution of a process. When used in Lean or Kanban software development environments, lead time refers to the length of time between when a piece of work gets added to the backlog and when it leaves the workstream of a team.

Lean A production and management philosophy derived in great measure from the Toyota Production System and the writings of Dr. W. Edwards Deming. In Lean, the focus is on organizing work and processes to maximize customer value while reducing inherent inefficiencies (waste).

Localizer / Internationalizer A language worker who specializes in adapting software for use in other languages and cultures.

Low Level Protocol Stack A protocol is a standard for communication between hardware and software. Individual protocols within a suite are often designed with a single purpose in mind. This modularization makes design and evaluation easier. Because each protocol module usually communicates with two others, they are commonly imagined as layers in a stack of protocols.

Minimal Marketable Feature / Minimum Viable Product - A conceptual feature or small feature set that is the minimum amount of value a customer would bother recognize and pay for. This is used in Agile and Lean Software development to encourage the development of only necessary functionality.

Pair Programming A technique or practice where two programmers work together at a station simultaneously, with one (the "driver") typing code, while the other (the "observer") reviews what was written. The roles switch frequently within the programming session.

Planning Game A game developed to help teams get over the emotional turmoil of planning their product. It specifically helps developers and business people collaborate more effectively Plugin A set of software components that add specific, customizable abilities to another, larger software application. These are commonly found in web browsers as a way increase functionality.

Pomodoro Technique A time management technique where working periods are timed, often using a visual or audio timer, and alternate with short break periods. Process Overhead The "cost", either real or virtual, of establishing and maintaining organizational processes.

Product Owner Creates the prioritized wish list of potential features that fill in a team's backlog prior to starting a software development cycle (sprint). This is a specific role defined by the Scrum development methodology.

Product Team A team dedicated to the end-to-end design, development and delivery of products or services. This is often associated with the creation of software, but is not exclusive to that industry.

Product Manager Responsible for eliciting software requirements and turning them into specifications for the software engineering group. In most organizations, the software product manager is responsible for creating User Acceptance Test (UAT) procedures, facilitating UAT sessions with end-users, and ensuring that the product meets the specifications and is deployed successfully.

Project Manager Key project management responsibilities include creating clear and attainable project objectives, building the project requirements, and managing the triple constraint for projects, which are cost, time, and quality (also known as scope). The Project Manager is the person ultimately responsible for the success and/or failure of a project and its deliverables.

Pull Systems in Lean, a pull system manufactures a product only when the customer needs or requests it. Pull systems are designed to ensure that wasteful overproduction rarely occurs.

Push Systems, in contrast, build large inventories of goods and wait for the market to consume them. Often these inventories are never sold or are sold at a discount when it is clear the market never needed the product in the first place.

Refactor A technique for improving the readability and reducing the complexity of an existing body of code without changing any of its external behaviors or functionality.

Regression Testing A type of software testing that attempts to identify if new problems are the result of changes to the software.

Retrospective A process or practice widely adopted in Lean and Agile methods that allows individuals or team members to reflect on completed work and identify both what worked well and what went wrong. They are usually conducted at regular intervals (daily, weekly, monthly) and encourage teams to continuously improve the quality of their work and collaboration.

Roadmap A visual way to communicate the entire scope of a project over the next two to three iterations. Provides a high-level and long-term reference for the evolutionary direction of a product or service.

Scrum Scrum is an iterative and incremental framework for project management mainly deployed in agile software development. The three fundamental roles in scrum methodology are Product Owner, Scrum Master and Team Member.

Scrum Master A specific role defined by the Scrum development methodology. An identified team leader whose job it is to keep everyone focused on the main goal during a sprint by removing obstacles to work and facilitating healthy communication and agile process flow.

Silo (vb, n.) The organizational and institutional structures that form around function, content/information, or expertise. Generally refers to the insularity of knowledge, teams and interactions that prevent collaboration.

Slack In project management, slack refers to the amount of time that a task in a project network can be suspended without causing a delay to:

⇨ subsequent tasks

⇨ project completion date

Software Development Lifecycle A phrase that encompasses and defines all of the tasks, activities and processes that go into developing and maintaining software.

Sprint Planning A key 'ceremony' in Scrum and Agile development during which the team identifies and totals 'estimation points' for each task in the backlog that will be completed during a given print period. The total points available to a team is generally derived from past performance or velocity. Read more at http://www.agilecollab.com/sprint-planning-meeting

Sprint Review A meeting with a set time limit that is used by Scrum teams to identify work that was completed and left unfinished and then present and demonstrated the finished work to key stakeholders or product owners.

Stand-up Meeting On each day of a sprint, the team holds daily meetings ("the daily scrum"). Meetings are typically held in the same location and at the same time each day. Ideally the daily scrums are held in the morning as they help set the context for the coming day's work. Daily scrums are strictly timeboxed to fifteen minutes. This keeps the discussion brisk but relevant.

Story Points In Agile software development methods, story points are used as an abstract estimate of the amount of work involved in a piece of work. Story points are typically based on a relative numbering scale like the Fibonacci sequence.

Stub In computer programming, a stub is a short program or routine that substitutes for a longer program or routine that is still in development. Stubs are often used as scaffolding during programming to enable progress in one area without having to complete all areas at the same time.

Swarming When a team or a group identifies a problem and collaborates (swarms) to solve it. Swarming is often used as a description when such collaboration is swift, immediate, and focused.

Swimlane A visual element used in process flow diagrams, or flowcharts, that visually distinguishes responsibilities for sub-processes of a business process. Parallel lines divide the chart into lanes, with one lane for each person, group or subprocess. Lanes are labeled to show how the chart is organized.

Technical Debt Code that was written and released with known defects that will require rework either when the fix becomes unavoidable. The more technical debt a product has, the more likely a catastrophic failure will occur.

Test/QA Software testing (often used interchangeably with Quality Assurance or just Testing) can be stated as the process of validating and verifying that a software program/application/product:

⇨ meets the requirements that guided its design and development;

⇨ works as expected; and

⇨ can be implemented with the same characteristics.

Test-driven Development A software development process where the developer first writes an automated test case to define a desired function or improvement, then writes and refactors code iteratively until it passes the test.

Tester A member of a software development team whose work it is to test changes made to the software by developers to verify that the changes work as expected, and to ensure that the changes have not introduced new issues.

Timebox (vb, n.) A technique or practice used in XP and Scrum to define work for specific development cycles.

Tribalism In a post-tribal society (i.e. modern context), the behavior and attitudes that stem from strong loyalty to one's own social group, as seen as a separate entity from "others".

Unit Testing In computer programming, unit testing is a method by which individual units of source code, sets of one or more computer program modules together with associated control data, usage procedures, and operating procedures, are tested to determine if they are fit for use. Intuitively, one can view a unit as the smallest testable part of an application.

(User) Acceptance Testing End-user testing of a product to ensure it is viable and delivers the value it promises.

User Interface In an information system, the User Interface (UI) is everything that has been designed for the human to interact with the system. This includes everything from the display to interactive peripherals like the keyboard and mouse.

User Interface Testing A form of software testing that focuses specifically on the functionality and usability of the user interface.

(User) Story In Agile software development methods, a user story is one or more sentences in the everyday or business language of the expected end-user of an application that captures what a user does or needs to do as part of his or her job function.

Value Stream Sequence of activities required to design, produce, and provide a specific good or service, and along which information, materials, and work flows.

Value Stream Mapping A visual mapping technique derived from lean manufacturing that is used to analyze and design the flow of materials and information required to bring a product or service to a consumer.

Velocity The measurement of story points completed over an iteration. An imprecise measure is used to communicate the amount of work a team is doing per Sprint.

Vision Any statement that creates a shared sense of the purpose, mission and values of a group, team, community, or organization

Waterfall A sequential design process, often used in software development processes, in which progress is seen as flowing steadily downwards (like a waterfall) through the phases of Conception, Initiation, Analysis, Design, Construction, Testing, Production/Implementation and Maintenance. Most projects are still managed this way.

Workflow An abstraction that allows real work-in-progress to be seen or identified as-it-happens. Workflow is usually demonstrated through some visual mechanism – either physical or digital – like a Visio flowchart or kanban board.

Zero Bug Bounce (ZBB) The point in the project when development finally catches up to testing and no active bugs currently exist. After zero bug bounce, the number of bugs should continue to decrease until the product is sufficiently stable for the team to build the first release candidate.

Zero Resolved Bugs (ZRB) The point in the project when there are no more Resolved bugs left to verify, i.e. when the testing team has verified all fixes that were done by developers. This is often a key milestone in waterfall-based software development that signifies the readiness of the release.

Common Abbreviations

TDD Test-Driven Development

PO Product Owner

PMO Project Management Office

PM Program/Project Manager

SDET Software Development Engineer in Testing

QA Quality Assurance

VP Vice President

CSM Certified Scrum Master

WIP Work-In-Progress

UI User Interface